How to Change to a Nongraded School

Madeline Hunter

Association for Supervision and Curriculum Development
Alexandria, Virginia

Association for Supervision and Curriculum Development
1250 N. Pitt Street, Alexandria, Virginia 22314-1403
Telephone (703) 549-9110   FAX (703) 549-3891

Copyright © 1992 by the Association for Supervision and
Curriculum Development. All rights reserved. No part of this
publication may be reproduced or transmitted in any form or by
any means, electronic or mechanical, including photocopy,
recording, or any information storage and retrieval system
without permission in writing from ASCD.

ASCD publications present a variety of viewpoints. The views
expressed or implied in this book should not be interpreted as
official positions of the Association.

Printed in the United States of America.

Ronald S. Brandt, *Executive Editor*
Nancy Modrak, *Managing Editor, Books*
Carolyn Pool, *Associate Editor*
Cole Tucker, *Editorial Assistant*
Gary Bloom, *Manager, Design and Production Services*
Stephanie Kenworthy, *Assistant Manager, Production Services*
Valerie Sprague, *Desktop Publisher*

$6.95
ASCD Stock No.: 611-92108
ISBN: 0-87120-193-3

Library of Congress Cataloging-in-Publication Data

Hunter, Madeline C.
    How to change to a nongraded school / Madeline Hunter.
        p.   cm.
    Includes bibliographical references (p.   ).
    ISBN 0-87120-193-3 : $6.95
    1. Nongraded schools.   I. Title.
LB1029.N6H86   1992
371.2'54—dc20   92-15765
                                                     CIP

How to Change to a Nongraded School

15.00

Preface

My introduction to the concept of a nongraded school occurred a quarter of a century ago when I read *The Nongraded Elementary School*, by John Goodlad and Bob Anderson (1959, rev. eds. 1963 and 1987). After reading the book, I complained to John, "What's so different about that? It's only what any good teacher does."

His response was, "Madeline, you are egregiously naive!"

I was. I had just finished creating a training school in inner-city Los Angeles, where my colleagues and I were diagnosing and prescribing for "at risk" students. We were using principles of learning to accelerate achievement and to provide a "custom tailored" program. We were determining worthwhile curricular goals and disciplining with dignity. We did all this at an intuitive level rather than making conscious and deliberated decisions on the basis of what research had shown to be most effective.

My current assignment was in the psychology department at the University of California-Los Angeles (UCLA). Goodlad invited me to become the principal at the UCLA Laboratory School to effect the metamorphosis of a rigidly graded school into a nongraded, team-taught school. "Why not?" I thought—and accepted the invitation with little notion of what would be involved in changing a school whose teachers had become well known for doing one thing and now would be required to learn some very different skills.

The first year was a nightmare. I have a Texas friend who maintains, "What doesn't kill you outright makes you stronger!" She is right. The staff and I survived that year, each learning from the other. By the end of the year, we had become a working team with most (but not all) respecting and learning from the skills of others.

Over our twenty years of work at the lab school, my colleagues and I discovered the power of deliberately incorporating principles of learning as we designed and implemented instruction. We learned the difference between trivial and worthwhile objectives. We learned the importance of teaching concepts, generalizations, and discriminations instead of only facts. We found that there is no single best way to teach nor a single best teaching personality. Most important, we learned that teaching is decision making.

Out of this crucible of experience grew our teacher decision-making model, now used worldwide. We found that every decision a teacher makes fits into one of three categories:

- *Content* (what is to be learned)
- *Learning behaviors* (what students will do to learn and to validate their learning)
- *Teaching behaviors* (what teachers can do to facilitate that learning)

In the years since we categorized teaching decisions, we have not found one decision that doesn't fit in those categories, regardless of the age, ability, or ethnicity of the learner; the content being learned; the model of teaching being utilized; or the school organization. Nongrading and team teaching simply brought into high visibility the professional knowledge, skills, and consequent decisions essential to an effective quality school.

The professional skills I have learned in order to articulate, demonstrate, and therefore transmit that knowledge resulted from the stimulation, dedication, and questions of a staff who became superb educational professionals. We were able to experiment with many different methodologies, knowing that the factor of teaching excellence was being held constant so that results could be directly attributable to the variable being investigated. This book is based on those experiments and experiences at the lab school.

How to Change to a Nongraded School (1) defines the nongraded school and describes its critical attributes; (2) explains what the nongraded school is designed to accomplish; (3) analyzes the organization of the nongraded school; (4) describes the placement of students in classes; (5) discusses planning of the curriculum and the instructional program; (6) identifies the necessary preparation of parents and teachers for a successful transition; (7) describes the reporting of students' progress as a result of successful nongrading; (8) analyzes the steps to independent learning; and (9) concludes with an account of how one traditional school became a nongraded and team-taught school with outstanding results.

* * *

I should list the names of every teacher and secretary with whom I worked at the lab school. Each person contributed to my growth both professionally and personally. One young teacher's aide who became a student teacher, then a teacher, supervisor, international consultant, and UCLA instructor in teacher education is Doug Russell. Doug was "brought up" in nongrading and team teaching by the outstanding teachers at the lab school. To him, I owe a special debt of gratitude for his review of this book and for making some excellent suggestions based on his knowledge from working with educators in the field.

I also owe special thanks to Sarah Kincaid and Cathy Dandridge for their graciousness as they translated my "airplane writing" into a manuscript and to Carolyn Pool for her assistance with the final manuscript.

—MADELINE HUNTER
University of California-Los Angeles

1
Critical Attributes of a Nongraded School

EDUCATIONAL PUBLICATIONS IN THE 1970S WERE JAMMED (AND damned) with accounts of three important innovations in education: continuous progress, nongrading, and team teaching. Not unexpectedly, the arguments for and against these innovations developed the usual heat, but without the necessary light. In the 1990s these same concepts again are emerging. Consequently, educators (and parents!) should be aware of what these "innovations" are and what they are not; what they were designed to accomplish and what they cannot possibly do. Let's take a look at each one.

What Is Continuous Progress?

Continuous progress refers to a student's progress from time of school entry until graduation. With continuous progress, students are challenged appropriately, according to their ability to master intellectual, physical, emotional, and social tasks at progressively more difficult levels. Continuous progress mandates that students should neither spend time on what they have already adequately achieved, nor proceed to more difficult tasks if they have not yet learned material or acquired skills essential to that new level of knowledge.

A major change has occurred recently in educational thinking. Formerly, *time* was the constant in schooling. Every student was given the same number of hours or weeks of class to "cover" a certain amount of material. The amount of *learning* actually accomplished became the variable. Some students learned a great deal, others learned less in that fixed amount of time.

We are now seeing a major paradigm shift. *Learning* has become the constant. We believe all students can, and should, accomplish stipulated kinds of learning to a satisfying degree. The variable, now, is the amount of *time* necessary for each student's success. Consequently, all students can be systematically progressing toward important, articulated educational goals. It will take some learners more time than others—but success is anticipated for all as a result of a student's effort; the assistance, encouragement, and expectations of competent educational professionals; and the time necessary for accomplishment.

A fine teacher, in any organizational environment, will generate a successful program. A nongraded organization increases educational possibilities and thus makes a successful educational environment more probable—*given skilled teachers*. Regardless of how the school is organized, teaching competence is the key to increased student learning.

I have defined teaching competence as the following attributes:

> (a) knowing research-based, cause-effect relationships between teaching and learning, (b) making instructional decisions based on that knowledge, (c) implementing those decisions while continually monitoring and, if indicated, adjusting on the basis of emerging data, including the results in students' achievement *during* and after instruction, and (d) synthesizing all of the above with skill and artistry, then, (e) evaluating-replanning after instruction.

What Is Nongrading?

Nongrading is an organizational plan that maximizes the possibility of continuous progress in the best available learning environment. Nongrading more nearly ensures that all students are learning in the best conditions possible at the level where their knowledge leaves off and new learning should begin. To create optimal learning opportunities, teachers group together students with an age range of 2 to 4 years, rather than homogeneously on the basis of age, ability, or grade level.

A graded school can be like a series of stair steps. Most students will spend a year on each step with students of the same age, then proceed to the next step. Progression has little relationship to what different students have learned, the environment in which they learn best, their needs for appropriate teaching and learning styles and methods, their speeds of learning, or their attitudes toward different academic tasks.

A nongraded school is like an inclined plane where progress can be continuous; thus, in the best educational environment available, each student proceeds at speeds and depths of thinking that are appropriate and generate success for that student. As a result, each student is more likely to be successful.

Let's examine the contrast between the extremes of a "traditional" graded school and an excellent nongraded one. As Figure 1.1 (page 4) shows, nongrading increases the opportunities for teachers to make productive accommodations to students' learning needs.

A nongraded school structure does not guarantee these differences, but nongrading makes them more possible. Making the differences more *probable* depends on a *continuing staff development program* that enhances the abilities of both beginners and skilled educators and provides the coaching necessary to translate ability into skilled, artistic practice. When a nongraded school also incorporates team teaching, students benefit even more from the collaboration of skilled educators.

What Is Team Teaching?

Team teaching is an organizational plan designed to maximize the effectiveness and artistry of each teacher for the benefit of every student. Team teaching is a way for two or more teachers to collaborate in planning, organizing, teaching, and evaluating instructional groups within a larger group. The resultant increase in learning options and professional skills makes it probable that each learner has the possibility of achieving more than if assigned to a self-contained classroom with a single teacher. Team teaching is simply "cooperative learning" at a professional level. Students, teachers, and parents realize increased "educational dividends" from it.

Figure 1.1
Contrasts Between Graded and Nongraded Schools

I. The Instructional Program

Traditional Graded School

A. Teacher follows text or curriculum guide by grade level and date.

B. Most of the time, all students work on the same task.

C. Teachers expect learning results to occur in a normal curve, "A" to "F."

D. Teachers teach by "activities" suggested in the text or curriculum guides.

E. The current instructional program may be isolated from what happened the year before or will happen after this year. Instruction is based on "things to teach in this grade."

F. The student's grade is determined by testing done at the end of a sequence of learning.

G. Paper and pencil is the major mode of testing.

H. Primarily, only language skills and math are subject to rigorous attention and evaluation.

I. Lessons are usually designed to produce only one level of learning outcome.

J. Teaching to achieve independent learners with a "zest for learning" is incidental.

Nongraded School

A. Teacher identifies long-range objectives, analyzes tasks, and then proceeds as rapidly as students' validated learning allows.

B. Students work on a task designed so that, with effort, each can realize satisfaction and success. Sometimes it's with the whole group, sometimes with a smaller, prescriptive group.

C. Teachers expect all students to earn an "A" or "B," but the time to do so will vary.

D. Teachers teach to instructional objectives that task analysis has indicated are essential to achieving the long-range goals.

E. The instructional program is based on a continuum that will lead to identified long-range goals.

F. Informal and inferential diagnoses, as well as formal testing, yield continuous contributions to instructional direction. The student's grade is a synthesis of many observations and measurements.

G. Frequent signaled answers; daily, brief oral and written responses; and student products are much more prevalent than formal tests.

H. All facets of a student's growth (intellectual, physical, academic, social, and emotional) are subject to rigorous attention and evaluation.

I. Lessons are designed with "educational wiggle," so a total group lesson will accommodate students' different "catch hold" points. If the lesson can't accommodate them, students are not subjected to expectations that are ridiculously easy or impossible to achieve. Often, students will work in appropriate subgroups.

J. Teaching to achieve independent learners with a "zest for learning" is a major outcome.

4

Figure 1.1—*Continued*

II. Expectations of Teachers

A. Teachers focus on a one-year view of students' progress.

A. Teachers focus on a long-term, developmental view that transcends the current year.

B. The major record of students' progress is the teacher's grade book.

B. Records become an individual student's portfolio of anecdotal observations, products samples, tests, and self-analyses.

C. Teachers assume major responsibility for what students do to learn.

C. Teachers *teach* students to become responsible partners in their own learning.

D. Staff development is optional.

D. Continuing staff development is a routine expectation.

III. Expectations of Students

A. Students judge their own achievement by comparison with others in the class.

A. Students judge their achievement by comparison with their own past record or with comparable students who have the same learning task and probability of success.

B. Students assume that if they're younger than the majority of the group, they're superior. If they're older, they've "failed."

B. Students are comfortable with students of different ages, with no ascriptions to their own competence.

C. Students feel little pressure for being responsible for their own learning. "It's the teacher's job to teach me."

C. Students realize that successful learning results from their own efforts in collaboration with teachers.

D. Students feel little responsibility for self-direction.

D. Students feel responsible for directing themselves, knowing when they understand, and, if they don't, doing something about it.

E. Students accept that they will "pass or fail."

E. Students know that they can learn if effort and necessary assistance are mobilized and that they are expected to do so.

IV. Composition of Classes

A. All students in the class, except "repeaters," are approximately the same age.

A. Students' ages vary from two to four years.

B. Classes may be tracked by ability or achievement.

B. Classes are composed to create an optimum learning environment for each member.

C. Students are assigned to a "grade" with certain academic expectations that are the same for all.

C. Students are assigned to a class judged to be the best learning environment. Expectations are the result of the diagnosed needs of members of the class, so that different learning tasks for different students will be expected.

Schools can be nongraded without team teaching—or team taught without being nongraded. Like apple pie and ice cream, they are separate, each good by itself. Together they make a wonderful combination: a true educational pharmacy of prescriptive alternatives.

What Nongrading Is Designed to Accomplish

To understand the organization of a nongraded school, let's first examine what it is *not*. Nongrading is *not* assigning students to classes because of intelligence or achievement. Schools with the brightest students in one class and the slowest in another are not "nongraded." Nongrading is *not* assigning good readers to one room and poor readers to another. Nongrading is *not* moving a student from one class to the next as soon as a certain topic or amount of work is finished. Nongrading is *not* randomly, or by necessity, combining grades in one classroom.

Now let's look at what nongrading is and how it facilitates continuous progress. As teachers make classroom placement decisions, nongrading necessitates a comprehensive diagnosis of many facets of each student that results in an educational, environmental prescription. This diagnosis is never considered to be final but is constantly being reassessed during instruction and, if necessary, modified. Out of this *continuing* diagnosis grow the scientific and artistic learning opportunities that are tailored to each student, then adjusted on the basis of emerging data: changes in the learner and in the learning situation.

This educational prescription is filled from the increased pharmacy of alternatives made possible by a nongraded school. A graded school provides fewer alternatives. Usually, Mrs. Smith's students are promoted to Mr. Jones' or Mr. Brown's room. In a nongraded school, the number of alternative placements for each student is increased because placements are not limited to one age or grade level. They are limited only by the creativity and competence of the staff. Typically, there will be several groups and several teachers to which each student could be assigned. Placement is selected to maximize the possibility of a challenging *and* supporting learning environment for each student. Staff members consider that student's position in relation to other students, as well as the individual student's needs for learning and teaching styles. In each class, teachers design the educational program to fit *those* students. This does not mean something different for every student, but a program appropriate for each.

Let's look at what this might mean in terms of a ten-year-old boy. If he goes to a graded school, he will be in the 5th grade; probably will have assignments (notice we don't use the word *learning*) in fractions, U.S. history, the 5th grade spelling book; and be playing 5th grade games. Next year, he and his classmates will move to another teacher's class, where, in most cases, they will be working with decimals and the 6th grade spelling book. All these activities should result from sensitive diagnosis with resultant prescriptive decisions, but too often in a graded school they might not.

Most of us would disagree with the use of astrology to determine students' assignments. Yet, this is what can happen in a graded school. The date of a student's birth can determine the learning environment and assignments rather than those factors, critical to the progress of each student, resulting from what is known about that learner. In a graded school, it is possible not to consider whether a student should move faster in math or repeat something not understood, whether a student has the skills necessary for complex team games or should be developing those skills.

With a fine teacher in any school organization, students will be diagnosed and the program tailored accordingly; but graded classrooms do not *mandate* such accommodation. Should the student have a less skilled teacher, that person probably proceeds conscientiously with the 5th grade material without considering whether it is an impossible learning task at this point or a waste of the student's time because it already has been learned.

With a graded class, it is as if a teacher were provided with age-ten clothes for all students in the class. These could be placed on students without considering whether they fit. As a result, some sleeves are too long, belts too tight, and shoulders droopy. General misfit or discomfort results, because ten-year-olds come in assorted sizes and shapes and no one size fits all.

In a nongraded school, to ensure continuous, efficient, and effective progress, a teacher must measure students' achievements and then adjust assignment "sizes" and expectations so they are appropriate. It is impossible to treat students as if all were the same. As a result, school tasks must be "fitted" so that each student will achieve as much as possible in each area. There is no such thing as the "average" student who will learn most with the "typical" program. Remember, *this does not mean something different for every student*, but academic assignments and instructional groups that are "fitted" to be appropriate for maximum progress of each learner.

Because of the flexibility of a nongraded school, the potential for students' achievement can be higher regardless of whether that achievement is measured by norm-referenced or criterion-referenced tests, or by observations— or by the satisfaction of teacher, parent, or student. Accommodations that more nearly ensure successful learning are implicit in the nongraded organization.

It is now believed that students have seven intelligences, not just one general "g" factor, as well as a need to be stimulated and encouraged to grow continuously in each. Howard Gardner (1983) has shown that students can vary in learning potential for linguistics, math-logic, physical, musical, and artistic skills, as well as interpersonal and intrapersonal abilities. Although the limits of each learner's potentials may be set by genetics, whether a student performs at the maximum or minimum of each potential depends on what happens after birth.

Curriculum and teaching need to take each of these intelligences into account. Of course, this should occur in any school organization, but it is more likely to occur in a nongraded school where the educational program is designed to accommodate the varying needs within each student. We need to continue to emphasize that taking differences into account does not mean something different for every student, but teaching that addresses the educational, social, emotional, and physical goals that are appropriate to and achievable by each student.

2
Organization of a Nongraded School

TYPICALLY, A NONGRADED ELEMENTARY SCHOOL INCORPORATES four major phases of schooling: early childhood, lower, middle, and upper elementary. Although each phase involves an interdisciplinary approach to learning, certain educational objectives have priority in each phase. A learner's progression from one phase to the next is based on a reasonable accomplishment of those prioritized objectives. Building self-esteem, an appreciation of one's own worth as well as the worth of others, is an overarching objective of all phases. Self-esteem is highly correlated with the increased academic, social, emotional, and physical accomplishments made more possible by skilled teachers in a nongraded organization. In addition, developing thinking skills at a level appropriate to each student is an embedded objective, regardless of content or phase of schooling.

In a nongraded school, art, music, literature, drama, and dance are considered to be as important and basic as the traditional "basics" and must therefore be included as important outcomes in all phases of schooling. Because the arts more easily accommodate differing levels of skills, teachers consider students' interests and talents in various forms of artistic expression when classroom placement decisions are made. Sometimes, the arts are relevant in grouping students in classrooms with teachers or students who will encourage and nurture special talents.

Early Childhood Phase

For the early childhood phase (typically ages four to six), the nongraded school has four prioritized objectives:

1. Developing reasonable autonomy.
2. Increasing language skills for working, playing, and learning productively with peers.
3. Working comfortably with appropriate materials and ideas.
4. Relating comfortably and appropriately to teachers.

If a child is comfortable with herself as a person separate from her mother and father; if she is comfortable with her peers and can interact productively, behaviorally, and verbally with a variety of other children; if she works comfortably with materials and ideas with only productive frustration or tension; and if she looks to adults for support and guidance but not for constant direction, that child has achieved the objectives of early childhood education and is ready to progress to the lower elementary phase. The early childhood phase includes a great deal of direct experience; and students develop skills in language, math, social studies, and science at appropriate levels, based on the collaborative judgment of both students and teachers. Students in this phase are encouraged to develop abilities in reading or computing; but skills in reading, math, and other traditional subject areas are not a determining factor in a child's progression to the lower elementary phase.

Lower Elementary Phase

Developing appreciation and skills in language, math, social studies, and science—as well as the arts—becomes a paramount objective at the lower elementary phase of schooling (usually ages five to eight). At this phase, students *must* develop the interests and academic skills so important to all future learning. The following are some objectives for the lower elementary phase:

1. Developing a firm base for fluency in language (reading, writing, listening, and speaking).
2. Developing facility and reasonable automaticity using operations in math to solve problems related to daily experiences.
3. Expanding skills in using information and observations to hypothesize, predict, and validate predictions.
4. Enhancing skills in working collaboratively with others.

Each phase of schooling has an age overlap with the phase before and after it (see Figure 2.1). For example, a six-year-old could be in either the early childhood phase or the lower elementary phase, depending on which environment is more likely (in the judgment of the teachers, parents, and student) to enable him to achieve the objectives he'll need for future success.

Likewise, if an eight-year-old were placed in the lower elementary phase of schooling, it is because he will profit from an environment designed to concentrate on and accelerate basic academic skills while developing self-esteem and leadership abilities.

Any continuing placement at one phase, therefore, is not considered a "failure" or retention. A student may work on the same level of reading, writing, and math as in the next phase, but benefit from an environment that is especially designed to accommodate her current social and emotional needs. Such a placement does *not* mean that she will have an extra year of elementary school. In fact, nongraded placement should eliminate that possibility.

Figure 2.1
Organization of a Nongraded School

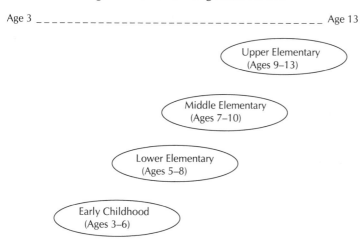

Age 3 _____ Age 13

Upper Elementary
(Ages 9–13)

Middle Elementary
(Ages 7–10)

Lower Elementary
(Ages 5–8)

Early Childhood
(Ages 3–6)

Note: Each phase may include several classrooms, each with students whose ages range two or more years apart.

Middle and Upper Elementary Phases

The middle elementary (ages 7 to 10) and the upper elementary phases (ages 9 and beyond), although involving much more complex interdisciplinary content, have the following target objectives:

1. Developing increasingly accurate self-evaluation: identifying and working on one's strengths, needs, and limitations.

2. Developing increasingly sophisticated learning strategies that will be effective in enhancing strengths and eliminating weaknesses.

3. Developing proficiency in learning processes and increasingly complex thinking skills.

4. Developing increasing self-propulsion in learning: becoming responsible for putting forth effort to enhance one's own learning.

5. Developing a "zest for learning" so that intrinsic motivation will more likely lead to life-long learning.

Although these same objectives are introduced, stimulated, and encouraged at the early childhood and lower elementary phases, they become major instructional targets, with accountability for achievement, in the middle and upper elementary phases of nongraded schools. All these outcomes are applicable to academic, artistic, physical, social, and emotional goals.

* * *

Though content at each phase becomes increasingly complex, knowledge of content is not just an end in itself but becomes the vehicle through which all school objectives are achieved. Teachers emphasize the interdisciplinary "threads" that unite the key concepts of each academic area, as well as the conceptual skills required of a mature learner. *The central goal of all schooling is the ability to understand, develop further, and use the results from humankind's creative approaches to studying and solving problems that are personal, societal, national, or global.*
If a student continues to fail to achieve the targeted objectives despite the teacher's best effort, staff members

place that student in a class that meets his needs for teacher style and peer group belonging. Keeping an academically nonachieving student with inappropriately younger, less socially and physically mature classmates is a violation of the principle of placement in the most enabling learning environment. He should be placed with appropriate age mates and given the best, for that student, teacher available. Then a special program can be designed to accommodate and alleviate his academic difficulties as much as possible. No organizational scheme is 100 percent successful 100 percent of the time. We don't expect nongrading to be.

3
Assigning Students to Classrooms

ASSIGNING STUDENTS TO EACH YEAR'S CLASSROOM GROUPS BEGINS
with a diagnosis of the phase of schooling that is most
appropriate for each student. For example, should the
student be assigned to the early childhood or lower
elementary phase? Nongrading provides many more
options than does a graded school because of the
combination of ages. Age is not the determining factor in
placement decisions; but it is essential that students are in
classes with some others of the same age. In that way they
don't regard themselves as different from where they think
they should be.

Decisions concerning the appropriate teaching style
and peer-group composition are considered as priorities in
each phase because these student needs do not change
rapidly. To optimize achievement, placement must be based
on information in six areas of a learner's development:
intellectual, academic, artistic, emotional, social, and
physical. Valid diagnosis comes from many observations, as
well as formal and informal assessments. Basing their
decisions on this information, educators will *estimate* the
following:

1. The most appropriate teacher(s) for this student, at
this point in the student's development

2. The composition of a group within which the student
might best learn

3. The type of stimulation in the educational
environment that will most likely increase motivation to
learn

4. The best instructional program within that
environment

Selecting Teacher(s)

The experience of every parent makes it obvious that the single most important factor in a student's school learning is the teacher's ability to promote that learning. Consequently, in a nongraded school, one of the first diagnostic questions is, "*At this point in time* (not forever!), what style of teaching is predicted to be most enabling for this learner?"

Should the student have a warm, supportive teacher who will encourage with words like "Oh, that's not hard—sit here and I'll work with you"? Or is this the kind of student who will relax and let the teacher do the work?

Would the student achieve better with a stricter, demanding (but not demeaning) teacher who says, "I expect that to be finished before you leave!" Or is this a student who cannot work well under such pressure? Or can this student function well with either support or demand, or both?

Should the student have a teacher who usually does things the same way so that what is going to happen can be anticipated? Or does the student find this predictability boring and need a great deal of variety to remain interested? Or can this student function successfully in either environment even though one may be preferred?

Parents know that what works with one child may be the worst possible thing for another. Scolding may make one brother reform and the other sulk. A great deal of excitement may cause one sister to rise to new heights while the other goes to pieces.

Students show the same difference in responses at school. The best teacher for Susie *at this time* may not be the best one for Johnny. In any school, it is important to determine the teacher most likely to be successful with the current needs and characteristics of each student, although those characteristics may vary at certain times or with particular activities. In graded schools, the selection of teachers is more limited because they are usually assigned to only one grade level of students.

Students don't come calibrated—and no standardized instrument has been devised to supply specific answers to the critical question of which might be the most productive teacher at a particular stage of the student's development. Experience has indicated that the eyes and ears of a sophisticated teacher can supply the most valid, *current* information available. By carefully observing and listening, a teacher can assess students' reactions to different ways of working with them and identify students who can direct their own learning and those who need support and guidance, those who "snap to" with strict instructions and those who rebel or are frightened. A relaxed atmosphere will reveal to an alert teacher which students thrive in such a climate and which take undue advantage of it.

Parents use the same informal, observational diagnosis to make wise decisions concerning whether to take action or ignore, whether to suggest or remain quiet, whether to intervene or leave alone, whether to help or insist on independence. Both teachers and parents realize that the correct action for one youngster may be inappropriate for another. This realization is an important basis for diagnosis and placement in a nongraded school.

The flexibility of nongraded classes is especially useful when new students are enrolled in the school. No attempt is made to do a complex advance evaluation of new students; teachers find it much more efficient to assign the child to the *middle* of a group and begin the diagnostic observation there. Because of the nongraded organization, it is seldom that a new student cannot be accommodated in the middle of a group that includes some age peers. As the student becomes known to teachers, subsequent placements can be made with greater precision.

Likewise, a new teacher's personality and abilities may not be known, although they may be inferred (but not always accurately) from an interview. Consequently, when a new teacher joins a nongraded school, students whose needs for a particular teaching style are not urgent may be placed in that teacher's classroom.

It is important that students who have a really intense need for a certain kind of teacher *not* be placed in a new teacher's group unless it is known that this teacher qualifies or that the student composition of a particular class group is more suited to that student's needs than an alternative placement would be.

With team teaching, there is little problem with a new teacher because the student can be assigned to a classroom on the basis of other teachers and students in the team. The new teacher can become a complement to the other professionals' personalities and skills and learn from them, while contributing to the richness of teaching styles and content knowledge.

An important by-product of this type of educational diagnosis is the knowledge that there is not one kind of "best teacher." Although all excellent teachers incorporate the same basic cause-effect principles of learning in their teaching, they may implement them in different ways or with different styles. Interestingly, as teachers observe and identify differing teaching styles and responses that are effective with certain students, they begin to add these styles and responses to their own repertoire of teaching skills. Students, *with appropriate instruction*, also learn to adapt to a variety of teaching styles. This adaptation contributes to a major objective of nongrading—that, eventually, each student will be able to function successfully because of, or despite, teaching style. Life does not custom tailor experiences to individual needs!

With the additional richness of personalities and skills made possible by team teaching, a student may start the year by working with the teacher who best matches the student's learning needs for all or most of the day. Then the student can gradually, in small "bites," learn to work productively with a different teaching style. "Weaning" should eventually result in reasonable comfort and achievement with all teachers in the team.

Learning from a team of teachers makes the student's accommodation to next year's teachers much more predictably successful. Although students will always have preferences, learning to learn regardless of teaching style is a major educational objective and has greater probability of being achieved when a team of teachers is involved. In this respect, the contrast to a one-teacher classroom is striking.

When working in a self-contained classroom, the teacher has the obligation to wean a student from dependence on one style of teaching: occasionally becoming less directive to a dependent student; possibly becoming more directive to an obstinate one; and becoming less supportive to students who want to lean on the teacher but who are ready for more independence. A central principle of professional service, rendering the service needed by the client, is one hallmark of an effective professional. But one teacher, working alone in an isolated classroom, must try to meet students' needs—and with little opportunity to learn from other teachers' styles. There should be variety of teaching styles at each level of schooling—for the growth of both teachers and students. Unfortunately, in the one-teacher classroom, teachers do not have the same opportunity as they do in teaming for the observational learning that results from seeing how other professionals respond to students and how students respond to different teaching styles and strategies. All teachers wish to be successful and work hard to accomplish that success. If given the opportunity, they will consciously (or unconsciously) begin to acquire additional skills in professional behaviors that they perceive as effective.

Selecting a Peer Group

After predicting which teacher(s) might be most successful with each student for the following year, staff members face the next diagnostic question in assigning students to classrooms: the kind of peer group that will contribute most to that student's learning *at this point in time.* As teachers extend their repertoires of teaching skills and responses to students, any one particular teacher becomes less critical to most students' success. Now, group composition becomes a more important factor in student placement. Should the student be socially, academically, emotionally, or physically at the top, bottom, or in the middle of the group, with close friends or making new friends? Which of these factors is most important to consider and accommodate at this stage of this student's development?

Meeting Students' Changing Needs

Students' needs—and their own self-perceptions—are in constant flux. Placement decisions should reflect these changes. For example, *at this point in time* (not forever!), should the student see herself as generally the most able, least able, or in the middle of the group? Will she work best with friends or be distracted by them? Does she need the security of old friends or the challenge of new? Will the addition of certain students to the group tend to increase or decrease learning effort? Academic achievement in any subject area is used only as a correctional factor; teachers ensure that each class includes a cluster of students with similar educational needs (gifted, remedial, social, physical, artistic, or emotional). This cluster is important because students learn from their peers as well as from the teacher; and, if possible, a teacher should not be caught with the inefficiency of developing a program for only one or two students. On the other hand, a class of only one kind of student (bluebirds, blackbirds, or buzzards) has been shown to be less effective than heterogenous classes.

In each phase of schooling, the peer group is never exactly the same each year. Every year, some students move to a new phase, some remain, and some are just entering that phase. Because of age overlap in the groups, usually there are several possible placements for most students. In this way, alternatives of teaching style and peer-group composition are always available.

Notice that I always use the phrase, "at this point in time," which implies that, as a result of instruction and circumstances, students' needs can change. To be effective, a nongraded program must more nearly ensure that, at graduation, a student will have accomplished more, not only academically but also by being able to learn with all kinds of teachers and in all kinds of groups.

Ensuring Variety in Custom-Tailored Groupings

In a nongraded school, depending on their needs, students are given the experience of learning while being the oldest, youngest, one of the more advanced students (academically, socially, physically, and emotionally), and one of the less advanced students. Students also experience being with friends and separated from friends as they progress through school. The teacher's goal is to develop in students increased resilience, effort, and resultant success, regardless of the learning environment: to develop self-propelled, successful, independent learners.

Parents often lament the stratification of their children's position in the family. The oldest may receive a great deal of attention from Mom and Dad, but the parents' expectations may have been too high and may have led to stress. Parents spend a great deal of time with the firstborn but, being novices, sometimes bungle the job.

The last born arrives in a family where there are other children as teachers and models. The parents are experienced and have more realistic expectations. They are not traumatized by the first illness or discouraged by the first problem. On the other hand, they may be tired of nursery rhymes, may have little desire to visit parks and zoos again, and may have lost interest in Scouting. The parents are older, more successful, busier, and have less time to spend on one child. How wonderful it would be if children could exchange positions in a family and take turns at being the oldest, youngest, and in the middle!

Obviously, this exchange is impossible at home; but at school it is not only possible but highly desirable. Students whose leadership ability quickly propels them to a position of prominence will need, at some time, to experience being with older, more powerful leaders, so they can develop the necessary ability to follow. Shy, reluctant students with leadership potential need to experience being one of the older, more capable members of the group, so they are encouraged and supported in developing skills they might be reluctant to try with their own age group. Once they have developed the necessary skills, they need opportunities to practice them, with support, in the many different kinds of groups that are made possible by a nongraded school.

Pairs of students who cannot function together need to develop immunity to another's ability to drain off their learning energy. Although teachers may begin by separating these children, eventual "immunization" must be tested by placing those students together again in a group, with the support necessary for them to continue functioning productively despite their distractor.

Conversely, certain students become too dependent on each other—what one wears, the other wears; what one thinks, the other thinks. Parents, educators, and psychologists agree that these students need to become more independent. Again, this weaning process may begin while they are in the same nongraded class working on different projects and in different instructional groups. Becoming an independent individual, however, is not complete until each can function productively in a class that does not contain the other, even though they may continue their friendship outside of class.

Charting the Placement of Students

One (not the only) way to deal with the logistics of assigning students to individual teachers or to teams is to set up pocket charts on tag boards or bulletin boards so that membership in class groups can be constituted, examined by teachers, and adjusted on the basis of each group's peer and instructional composition. The teachers for the following year are listed at the top of each group with probable age ranges.

Each student's name is placed at the top of a small card that can be inserted in the class identified on the pocket chart. Relevant data are listed on the card: age, physical-social-emotional maturity, important academic achievement and needs, as well as any special considerations, assets, or liabilities that should be accommodated in next year's placement.

These cards give flexibility to the manipulation of groups, with teachers and administrators composing and changing them to create the optimal next year's educational environment for each student.

The following are examples of student data that are considered when teachers form groups. Teachers who know the student record only terse phrases on the card, but they can be translated into the following information:

> Bill is physically large for an eight-year-old, a potential leader, average in math, less able in reading and writing skills. He needs to be in a class with friends his size who also need skilled teaching that will stimulate them to put forth more effort to acquire language and math skills and to make more advanced math skills meaningful. There

need to be opportunities in the group to develop his potential for leadership; so he should not be overshadowed by students who already are very skilled and popular leaders.

Recorded on the card would be: "Bill, 8 yr.–4 mo., big, math OK, lang. ?, push academics, leadership with friends."

Tom is an acknowledged leader. He needs to be in a group with other strong leaders so he can learn the skills of supporting others and not always be "in charge." He needs an instructional group whose academic needs are similar to his, so that with and from peers he will be encouraged to accelerate his own academic growth through cooperative endeavor.

Recorded on his card is: "Tom, 11 yr.–3 mo., leader, needs follower skills, cooperative learning, self-direction in academics."

Carol, a bright girl whose mother neglects her, needs to feel valued by both adults and friends. Consequently, the most important aspect of her placement is that she be in a group where she feels that *when she puts forth effort* her contributions will be valued and important to peers and teachers. She has average academic skills, and she needs an appropriate peer group to which she can make productive contributions. In this way, she can realize her responsibility for the increased effort that goes with earning respect and loyalty from others.

On the card: "Carol, 8 yr.–7 mo., needs approval, average skills, learn to put forth effort with similar students." Although Carol's paramount need at this point is to feel valued, increasing her social *and* academic skills is essential to fulfilling that need. Therefore, she is best placed in a group where, with high expectations, support, and effort, she will be encouraged to make important contributions and be perceived as a valued group member.

Suzanne is a deliberate but steady learner. She needs to be in a group where others also need more redundancy and practice. A teacher who makes sure one thing is well learned before proceeding to the next is essential to her steady growth. As long as she is with some friends with the same needs for deliberate pacing, she is likely to make steady, if slow, predictable growth. She is a social, friendly child and will "get along" regardless of other personalities, but she needs a teacher who will check for objective evidence that one thing is well learned before proceeding to the next.

Recorded on the card is: "Suzanne, 7 yr.–8 mo., steady, needs much practice, good social skills, important to validate learning."

Seldom is there the perfect placement for every student. The best approximation can be achieved as tentative placements for the following year begin in March, but are examined, adjusted, and corrected through April and May. In this way, the optimum personal, social, emotional, and educational environment is estimated, selected, and corrected by many professionals. Teachers who have worked with the students in current and past years are sensitive to each student's needs; but they also are aware of the reality and limitations of what is currently available. Nongraded schools try to custom tailor the environment for each student, but students also need to develop necessary strengths as they learn to adapt productively and perform well in a less-than-perfect environment.

Timing of Classroom Assignments

Classroom assignment is usually for one year. Students are not moved as soon as they have finished one book or set of materials; there is no ceiling on the amount of learning possible in any group. On rare occasions, students are moved to a different group during the year if, for emotional or social reasons, their needs in these areas change and can be better met in a different group. Occasionally, students wear out their welcome in one group and need to be given a fresh start in a new group with a teacher who is prepared to make this placement more successful.

Placements for the following year are usually made in late May; however, professional deliberation for those placements begins much earlier. During the first weeks of the new school year, placements are carefully checked to be sure there has been no unanticipated change in the student during the summer. Seldom do teachers need to correct a placement, because it is based on the more stable needs for learning environment rather than on academic achievement.

Involving Parents in Decisions About Classroom Assignment

Educators need to explain to parents the reason for their child's placement in a classroom or group, show parents how the school environment is deliberately custom tailored to optimize their child's achievement, and actively invite their suggestions and observations. Most parents' reactions are, "I didn't realize you knew my child so well!" Of course, some parents have preferences for certain teachers or groups; and when those needs are not met, the parent is entitled to know the reasons that resulted from careful, professional consideration. Educators should listen to parents' reasons for requests and use this valuable information in placement decisions.

In late spring, teachers may find it helpful—and politically adroit—to send parents a questionnaire in which they can give their impression of the *kind* of teacher and group (not *which* teacher) with whom they believe their child will best learn. The questionnaire should be tailored to the particular parent population of the school. The survey should request whatever information the educators think will be helpful and should be phrased so that the vocabulary is appropriate and the intent is clear to parents (see Figure 3.1 for a sample questionnaire).

Another important outcome of creating the questionnaire is that the process helps the school staff clarify and articulate information that is needed and used for placement.

Figure 3.1
Parent Questionnaire

Dear Parents:

As we assign students to classrooms and to teachers for next year, your impressions of your child's needs are very important to us.

Please answer the following questions to give us your perception of the school environment that will contribute most to your child's academic, emotional, and social growth. On the back of the questionnaire, add any additional information you wish us to have.

Child's name _____ **Date** _____

Parent's name _____

Does your child work best:

- In an environment that is predictable, so the child knows what will happen? Or does he or she need changes and variety to stay interested?

- When your child knows exactly what is expected in performance, or does that make the child anxious or bored?

- When your child can easily get help, does that make the child feel more secure, or will she or he take less responsibility for self-direction?

- When your child feels comfortable as an adequate member of the group, or will the child put out more effort if others can do better?

Other questions:

- At this time, does your child need to learn how to become more cooperative or more assertive?

- What do you most hope your child will accomplish next year?

- Place additional information on the back of this sheet.

Thank you for your help!

The Staff of _____School

4
Designing the Instructional Program

AFTER STAFF MEMBERS AT A NONGRADED SCHOOL *TENTATIVELY* determine the optimal teacher and peer-group assignments *at this point in time* for a particular learner, teachers in the assigned self-contained or team group then consider the appropriate instructional program for that group. The reason this question comes last is that specific classroom organization and learning tasks are more easily adjusted than are class composition and learning environments. It may be difficult for a teacher to change teaching styles and responses if different ones are needed by particular students. (As an extreme example, a female teacher cannot be a father figure to a boy who needs one.) Also, peer groups cannot become different because a student needs them to be.

Once the classes or teams are constituted, the teacher or the team designs a specific instructional program, based on district and school goals, as well as students' needs. This program is dynamic in that it continues to be responsive to the changing needs of students as they progress.

Curriculum of a Nongraded School

The critical attribute of any defensible curriculum and instructional program is that it specifies in perceivable terms important goals and objectives for each major academic, aesthetic, social, emotional, physical, and intellectual strand to which the time and energy of teachers and students will be directed. The program also provides a continuum of objectives that have high probability of enabling students to predictably proceed toward achievement of those goals.

In a graded school, checkpoints in each sequence are assigned to grade levels (addition and subtraction without regrouping in 1st grade, division of fractions in 5th grade, etc.). Typically, teachers use the graded text and workbook activities created by people who have little idea of the major interdisciplinary curricular strands of the school or the prior knowledge and abilities of students in each class. Some of these activities ("Answer the questions at the end of the chapter," "Make a word map of the desert," "Fill in the blanks"), used routinely, may coincidentally contribute important understanding and skills *if* the teacher ensures that those connections are made by students. For the most part, students view those activities as isolated assignments with no relevance for problem solving, creativity, or decision making in future schooling or in life. As one boy commented after doing a workbook page on subject-verb correspondence, "I is finally finished!"

In a nongraded school, students are diagnosed concerning their achievement along each continuum of the curriculum. They are taught by whatever teaching model is deemed appropriate (cooperative learning, computer-assisted instruction, discovery, direct teaching, etc.), their learning is validated, and then they focus on the next content or skill that will move them closer to the terminal goal, thereby more nearly ensuring their continuous progress toward successful achievement. Because teachers in a nongraded school know the long-range curricular goals at an articulate rather than an intuitive level, they are better able to help students build connections from past work into present assignments and then to future goals. ("As we learn about our own needs in our community, you will find you can apply those same categories of human needs as you later study the explorers in our state history or, in fact, the people of any country in any time period.")

We are, of course, identifying the qualities of excellent teaching that can (and do) occur in any school organization with a skilled teacher. Nongrading does not guarantee teaching skill. A nongraded organization simply highlights the necessity for excellent curricular and pedagogical judgments, thereby increasing the probability they will occur. That probability results from many staff meetings where, from the district curriculum, teachers develop and refine goals and objectives. As a result, teachers become sensitive to the reasons for students' expending time and energy on achieving particular content, skills, processes, and attitudes—rather than dissipating time and energy on nonrelevant busywork assignments that happen to be available in books and practice sheets.

Selecting an Interdisciplinary Theme

In planning the instructional program for a self-contained classroom, the teacher's most difficult decision may be selecting an interdisciplinary theme or social studies unit that will accommodate all students. With a teaching team, usually there is one social studies unit for the whole team; and students are grouped with different teachers to accommodate learning styles and interests, as well as academic and social needs. Occasionally, a team will elect to have more than one social studies unit so that students or teachers may select the one they need.

Obviously, interdisciplinary, thematic instruction is valuable; however, to accommodate a district's mandated social studies curriculum, content can be "leap frogged." If state history is scheduled for the 4th grade, U.S. history for the 5th grade, and world history for the 6th, each content area may be taught to the total group in succeeding years in a way that is comprehensible to and achievable by each student. Key concepts and generalizations are applicable to all history studies and can be learned in any historical context. Initially, this approach will be difficult for teachers who are accustomed to teaching names, dates, and battlegrounds. Interdisciplinary, thematic instruction in a nongraded classroom is a skill that, with staff development, teachers will "grow into."

Accommodating Varying Levels of Academic Ability

Some people may argue that 4th graders can't read the 6th grade textbook. But neither can some 6th graders, and the more able 4th graders can easily read the text. In the same way that a skilled teacher accommodates poor readers in the 6th grade by reading with or to them, putting the chapter on tape, rewriting material, or pairing students for cooperative learning, so will the skilled nongraded teacher accommodate the special needs of students with lower ability levels.

In the same way that a sophisticated teacher in a graded school extends and enhances the assignment for the more able students (not more of the same, but a qualitatively different task), so will the skilled nongraded teacher modify the assignment for more advanced and gifted students regardless of their age or grade level.

As an example, if students are studying the Civil War, the more able students may read conflicting material (possibly about the Lincoln-Douglas debates) and be ready to persuasively present the arguments of either side. This gives them experience in dialectical thinking: taking the strongest, supportable position against their own point of view.

The students with average abilities may read the chapter and work individually, in pairs, or in cooperative groups to prepare for a discussion of the issues or about questions presented by the book or by the teacher.

The teacher may work with other students, regardless of their grade level, who would have difficulty reading or understanding the material. This "teacher's group" may read together or listen to the teacher read while they follow in their books, supplying the word when the teacher pauses to ensure they are following the print (a good way to practice reading!). After each meaningful part, the group constructs discussion questions to present to the total group and anticipates what would be acceptable contributions. Even if they can't finish the whole chapter in the time allotted, they will truly understand the material they have covered. This knowledge will give them a firm foundation for the additions of the unread material through other students' contributions. With this "advance organizer" of the information in the remainder of the chapter, students at lower levels of ability will probably read it later without assistance.

Then, with the total group, the teacher's group presents their discussion questions and possibly conducts the initial discussion. The teacher's group is also responsible for asking clarifying questions (a skill they should have learned and practiced in a previous instructional group) or for restating the concepts or generalizations in different words.

Finally, or during the discussion, the advanced group may summarize, provide additional information, or present the persuasive arguments and beliefs of both the Union and of the Confederacy, answering the questions or concerns posed by the others.

Cooperative learning is an additional, excellent instructional technique with a heterogeneous group *when appropriately used with students who have been adequately prepared to engage in it.* In a group that includes a combination of abilities, each student has responsibility for contributing to and participating at an appropriate "catch hold" point, while learning from peers with different catch-hold points. Students who cannot achieve independently are assisted by and learn from others as they become responsible and accountable for understanding the content. Students with greater abilities have assignments that tap and tax their abilities, as well as give them appropriate responsibility for contributing to the level of understanding of the total group.

Custom-Tailoring Assignments

Each student, regardless of ability or interest, has a right to special, custom-tailored assignments, as well as the responsibility for contributing to the total group. At times, students should select a preferred task from a repertoire of alternatives designed by themselves or by the teacher.

Although this customizing can be done in any classroom, it is *required* in the nongraded school. As teachers gain experience with custom tailoring, they increase their skills in designing learning opportunities with "academic wiggle" that will accommodate diverse, larger groups rather than only one level of student ability. For example, in a history lesson, students with lower levels of ability may contribute information about Washington, students with higher levels may identify the issues that separated the Colonists from England, and skilled students may extrapolate to current civil rights issues. Then, in cooperative groups or in a total group, each student has the opportunity *and obligation* to participate in and learn from all three contributions. Learning time can be maximized by total group discussions, which encourage interaction, extension, and clarification yet accommodate different levels of thinking and achievement.

For a historical fiction unit, students might select books that range from *Ben and Me* (3rd grade reading level—about the mouse who told Benjamin Franklin how to invent wonderful things) to *Gone With the Wind*. (Adult novels that are not on the school list need to be approved by the student's parent.) Students will then write a brief summary of characters, setting, plot, and problem resolution. Also, according to their abilities, they will do a research report to determine the historical accuracy of their book. Finally, they may plan and present a report to their group.

In math, while some students are learning number facts, concepts, or operations *with meaning attached*, students with higher levels of ability can be creating meaningful applications of these operations, concepts, and generalizations to the social studies, language, and science content being studied by the class. In this way, skilled students contribute to the transfer of mathematical understandings and concepts to the total curriculum.

In a nongraded class, the teacher may work with the total group or with cooperative groups to enable all students to make responses at a level appropriate to their particular stage of learning. Listening to a story, viewing a film, painting a picture, participating in a discussion, practicing what has been taught, and creative writing are examples of activities that can accommodate students' responses, from simple participation to highly complex cognitive and creative involvement.

When a particular assignment will accommodate only one level of response, the teacher will work with smaller subgroups or design cooperative groups composed of those students for whom the assignment is appropriate. Multiplying fractions, learning a specific spelling list, independently reading a certain book, and analyzing particular written materials are examples of learning tasks that must be neither too hard nor too easy to accomplish for the students assigned these tasks. When cooperative groups are working on such an assignment, the anticipated outcomes must be productive, but could be different for *each* member.

Diagnosing Students

In determining the learning task on which each student should be working, we must acknowledge that the student's age and number of years in school will not tell us the answer. Assessing what a student knows and next needs to learn results from skilled observation, formal and informal testing, or sophisticated inference. Many learning tasks are sequential in their order of difficulty. You have to be able to count with understanding before you can add and subtract. Those skills precede multiplication and division. Trying to teach an advanced skill before a student has mastered necessary preliminary skills is not only a waste of time, but it retroactively interferes with the learning that already has been achieved and convinces the student that there is no use putting forth further effort. It is like trying to place the fifth row of bricks in a wall when the third and fourth are not in place. The whole wall is apt to collapse.

All students have peaks and valleys in their achievement. One may be a fine reader but weak in mathematics. Another may write a great story, but with atrocious spelling. Teaching as if all of a student's learning were at one grade level is ineffective, for it neither brings up learning valleys nor enhances peaks. This variation in achievement levels is one of the many reasons that tracking doesn't work. The "best" students aren't all the same or always the best in every subject. Teachers must assess students' knowledge and skills in each subject separately. When assessment reveals the points of appropriate difficulty, teachers can focus students' learning efforts where they're needed, using many different modalities. Again, this diagnostic and prescriptive accommodation should occur in every type of classroom, but nongrading makes the process impossible to ignore.

To determine instructional groups with a dependent sequence of learning (addition and subtraction before multiplication and division, writing sentences and paragraphs before writing essays and reports, mastering simple concepts before more complex generalizations), teachers must diagnose their students to find out where new learning needs to begin.

There are three types of diagnosis: formal, informal, and inferential.

Formal Diagnosis

A formal diagnosis is a carefully constructed evaluation instrument (not an "off the top of my head" group of questions or problems) that gives accurate information about students' current levels of achievement. Unless it is a published instrument, an effective formal diagnosis takes a great deal of time to construct (but can be saved and used in the future). Formal diagnostic instruments take additional time to administer and time to correct. Sometimes such a test gives too much information so that much of it becomes obsolete before it can be used by the teacher. The advantage of formal diagnosis, done well, is its accuracy. The disadvantage is its cost in the time and energy of both teachers and students. Other types of diagnosis are more time efficient.

Informal Diagnosis

Often an informal diagnosis is sufficient. Informal diagnosis results from answers (signaled or oral) to diagnostic questions or *brief* written answers or observations of students' activities, processes, or products in a specified, less extensive learning area. Informal diagnosis requires planning but has several advantages over formal diagnosis:

1. Informal diagnosis requires little class time (often it occurs while teaching or introducing a new subject).

2. It provides immediate information (no waiting until that night or the next day for results).

3. Done well, informal diagnosis usually is accurate enough to let the teacher know whether students are ready to move on or need more practice or reteaching.

Informal diagnosis has several disadvantages. First, it requires fast perception and processing by the teacher.

Inexperienced teachers may not be able to process the emerging information swiftly and accurately. Second, when skillfully done, informal diagnosis can be reasonably accurate and time efficient but sacrifices some of the accuracy and depth provided by formal diagnosis. Third, informal diagnosis doesn't provide the objective baseline record necessary to validate progress.

The following are some examples of effective informal diagnosis. First, to diagnose writing skills, teachers can ask students to write a paragraph (or page) about themselves as learners, about what they like to do, or play, or learn. Anything the teacher is sure students know will reveal students' abilities in written expression. To be avoided are topics where information may not be possessed by some students (e.g., community, Washington, pollution). Those topics will not constitute a valid writing diagnosis from an uninformed student.

Second, in some subjects, a *signaled diagnosis* conducted verbally with the whole class often gives quick and reasonably accurate beginning information. For example, the instruction "Make a plus, minus, multiplication, or division sign with your fingers to show the operation you would use to solve this problem" will give initial information about students' ability to select the correct operation in word problems. "Point to your forehead if this is true and to the floor if it is false. Do nothing if you're not sure," can indicate students' factual knowledge. "Make a 'P' with your fingers if this is a phrase, a 'C' if it is a clause" can give a reasonably accurate initial diagnosis. The possibilities are limited only by a teacher's professional knowledge and creativity. Have students close their eyes if you want to avoid "plagiarism." From the front of the room, it's easy for the teacher to spot those who need to "take a little peek." That also becomes important diagnostic information.

Students' signaling is only one of the quick and efficient ways of doing an initial diagnosis. The elimination of hours of test correcting provides time to design more effective and inspired learning opportunities. Because all such informal diagnosis is continually refined, corrected, and reassessed while teaching, the initial diagnosis does not have to be perfect.

On the basis of students' responses, either verbal (oral or written) or by body language, a teacher is continually making one of four professional decisions:

1. Move on, the students know it.
2. Give more practice, they need it.
3. Go back and reteach, they don't know it.
4. Abandon ship, today's not the time.

On a windy, rainy Friday afternoon or on the day of the carnival, dance, or big game, the "abandon ship" decision may be the most professionally sophisticated decision. Also, when there is much confusion, the best strategy is to stop, let students' "dust of confusion" settle until the next day, and spend some time that evening designing a better planned and more predictably successful lesson.

Inferential Diagnosis

Inferential diagnosis is very time efficient. It takes only fleeting thoughts from a teacher's memory. An inference is a judgment about the present based on knowledge from the past. That judgment is only as accurate as the match between the present and the past. A teacher "knows" that typical 5th grade students already have learned that Lincoln was president during the Civil War, have learned their addition and subtraction facts, and are able to write a simple paragraph. Therefore, teachers probably will not diagnose for this information or skill. Only when ongoing performance reveals that a student lacks these inferred skills will a teacher diagnose that student as needing remediation that supplies the missing elements.

That same 5th grade teacher will infer that students are not facile with common denominators and will probably start teaching that content with no prior diagnosis. Inferred diagnosis has the advantage of requiring little time for either teacher or student. Its disadvantage is that current students may not match those of the past; and errors of underestimating and overestimating can be common, resulting in student confusion or boredom if the inferential diagnosis is not quickly validated or revised by formal or informal diagnosis.

Diagnosis and Evaluation—A Complementary Process

Diagnosis and evaluation are the same processes, but their purposes are very different. Diagnosis is the process of gathering information to determine the degree of learning so that the teacher can plan specific learning opportunities that will assist the student in successful achievement of the intended learning outcome. Evaluation uses the same process but *may* gather data with more precision to make a classification judgment about a student's current achievement to determine a grade, an honor, or a placement. Evaluation requires objective evidence to support that judgment. Informal or inferential diagnoses do not yield the necessary empirical evidence.

Any initial diagnosis is a rough cut that will continually be refined as the teacher monitors each student's progress. For initial diagnosis in math, students may be given a variety of problems to see which they can solve and which skills they need to learn. From each student's performance, tentative instructional groups are formed. These groups are not a "year's sentence" but will frequently change as content, objectives, and students' achievements change. Refinement and correction of diagnosis is a continuing process based on the growth in students' performance that results from skilled teaching.

Teachers constantly monitor the results from students' assignments to cooperative groups or to specific instructional groups and continually adapt such assignments and groups, as much as possible, to particular students' current needs. These changes do not occur daily or even weekly; but as students' needs and interests develop and change, so do the assignments of whole classes or smaller instructional groups. There is nothing static in a nongraded class.

Such complex assessments and accommodations sound like a tremendously difficult job. It is, but sensitive diagnosis is essential to effective teaching—and the excellent teacher accomplishes it daily in any school organization. Teachers who put forth the effort will find it is possible to learn and effectively practice this essential professional skill if they are given the necessary staff development. Such learning begins with an awareness that individualized or custom-tailored instruction does not mean a different task for every student but objectives and activities that are appropriate for each student. Even if individual, tutorial service were possible, it would not be desirable for most students. In a group, the student has the advantage of learning a great deal from others as well as from the teacher; and it is a learning mode that will occur throughout life.

Teaching in a nongraded classroom is not different from teaching effectively in any classroom. On the basis of formal, informal, or inferred diagnosis, the effective teacher selects (or delegates that selection to students) an instructional objective that may or may not be communicated to students, depending on whether that information will be enabling or deterring to achievement. (How many students will react positively to, "Today you will learn punctuation," or "multiply binomials," or "improve your behavior in the cafeteria"?) That famous (or infamous!) "lesson design" that we developed at UCLA (to help teachers *plan* instruction) identified what a teacher must *think* about in designing a learning opportunity, *not* what must be present in every lesson. Any administrator, supervisor, or peer who observes and analyzes a teacher's performance by using a checklist of "what should occur" *does not understand teaching.* An astute observer never looks for the presence or absence of anything, but analyzes the appropriateness, effectiveness, and artistry of what is occurring.

Initial Planning of the Instructional Program

Before school starts in the fall, the individual teacher or teaching team examines unifying curricular threads and *tentatively* plans the major curricular outcomes for the year, sketching in component objectives that will predictably lead to those outcomes and identifying enabling materials (print, video, computers, etc.). The qualifier "tentative" is important because teachers are constantly building in detail and correction as their continuing diagnoses reveal students' needs for adjustment and accommodation. No curricular plan is set in cement, but is modified by sensitive, ongoing assessment in response to emerging data.

This information includes the accomplishments, interests, needs, and behavior of students, as well as current issues from the outside world.

As a result, teachers cannot "run off" all their follow-up work in the summer. They can tentatively plan assignments; but custom tailoring occurs as the teacher ascertains the needs of these particular students and builds in necessary extra practice, remedial assignments, and enriching activities in a way that most effectively enables students to reach the desired goals and objectives.

Initial planning also includes opportunities for students to set their own goals. Students often will make content decisions and determine their own way of learning. Teachers must ensure that students' time in school is spent productively by enabling students to *educationally self-actualize*, not just put in time with irrelevant activities or busywork.

5
Appraising Program Effectiveness

IN A NONGRADED SCHOOL, ASSESSMENT OF STUDENTS' ACHIEVEMENTS (intellectual, academic, psychomotor, social, and emotional) is continuous. Norm-referenced standardized tests will not give the information necessary for a nongraded instructional program. Both formal and informal assessment measures (anecdotal records, products, portfolios, criterion-referenced tests, self-assessment) should continually be used to monitor progress, to modify plans or curriculum, and to indicate new directions. Designing teacher-initiated, informal, effective assessment measures is a complex professional skill that should be developed and practiced in a series of staff development meetings. Most teacher preparation programs do not include adequate assessment skills.

Validating Student Learning

Having well-articulated instructional objectives, both short and long term, simplifies the process of assessment. An objective like "The student will name the capital of each state" not only is hard to justify, but takes a very different and much simpler type of assessment than "The student will define a state and explain the function of a capital." Defining what is to be learned and objectively determining that it has been learned is essential to all successful teaching and mandatory in a nongraded group. In a nongraded school, teachers can't just *hope* a student has learned; they must base subsequent instructional decisions on valid *evidence* of that learning. This process of validation is one reason that students have the possibility of learning more in a successful nongraded school. They don't proceed to more difficult learning tasks without acquiring *essential* prior knowledge and skills. Rather than slowing students down, the process of confirming their knowledge accelerates their achievement. As a result, they will achieve more—and make higher test scores.

Reporting to Parents

Even when a report card must be used, teachers should hold conferences with parents two or three times a year to report each student's progress through the four phases of schooling. Teachers need to report *to* parents, as well as gather relevant information *from* them (Hunter 1978). In each conference, information and statements are documented by the student's specific behavior or products in academic, social, emotional, physical, and artistic endeavors. A parent might be told:

> Bill can solve problems using all the operations in math. Now, he needs to become more comfortable in applying his knowledge to new situations. For example, he can do long division easily, but he was perplexed when he needed to compute his number of words per minute in our reading speed test.

The importance of the student's ability to deal with learning tasks also needs to be reported:

> Mary is comfortable when she is working with familiar material. We are going to help her move toward new ideas and processes with less concern about her immediate performance. She is bright and able and needs to learn that when she puts forth effort she will be successful.

Because parents have learned to assess their child's achievement through grades, initially it may be difficult for them to interpret statements regarding their child's needs and achievements described in behavioral terms. Therefore, the teacher is responsible for reporting, in terms that are meaningful to each parent, the student's satisfactory progress, or lack of it, with defensible reasons, along with what will be done to accelerate future learning. Parents who are dissatisfied with the clarity of reporting in a conference may have been given accurate information—but not in a language they could understand, based on their previous knowledge and experience.

Teachers need to develop both skills and artistry in parent conferencing. The school should provide a series of staff development meetings with subsequent practice and coaching in how to give parents *accurate* knowledge of the progress of their child, as well as how to guide parents in reinforcing or accelerating that progress at home. Making parents collaborators is an important outcome of nongraded schools (see Chapter 6, "Preparation of Parents").

Frequent communications between school and home are essential to keeping parents informed between reporting periods. Although teachers' notes and phone calls are sometimes indicated, students, themselves, should assume much of this responsibility. They can use a portfolio—a large brown envelope bearing the student's name and decorated to symbolize the student—to keep a weekly collection of representative work and "diagnoses" of what was especially pleasing to them, satisfactory, or in need of additional effort or help.

When parents know that this portfolio is coming home on a certain day each week (or every two weeks), they can plan time to discuss it with their child and, as a result, feel they are well informed of their child's progress. The student also has the practice of objectively evaluating and communicating, "How am I doing?"

If appropriate, parents can indicate in writing their participation in the weekly or bimonthly student-parent conference and send back to the teacher any questions they may have, with the portfolio being the "mailbag."

Formative School Assessment

A total school appraisal should be systematically planned and implemented at least every other year as a formative guide to validate or modify the school program. Often a central office specialist or a university consultant can give valuable advice and set direction.

Formative evaluation begins with specified and perceivable long-term outcomes that are agreed upon by the school staff. These outcomes also must be congruent with district and state outcomes. If there is disagreement concerning the appropriateness of either school, district, or state outcomes for a particular group of students, that disagreement needs to be articulated, examined, and resolved by the professionals involved, *not* ignored.

With "at risk" students, regardless of the cause, a task analysis will reveal en route objectives that will bring students closer to the desired outcomes. Those students, given time and skilled instruction, also can eventually achieve reasonable success.

A special advantage of the nongraded school is that there are no static objectives and expectations for every member of the class as there tend to be in a graded classroom. As a result, students can move comfortably toward the desired outcome. An expectation is that all outcomes will be reached at different times by different students.

Periodic evaluation, formal and informal, is essential to all schooling. No longer can we "hope they know"; we must secure objective evidence of students' progress.

We also must validate that progress is toward agreed-upon objectives. This does not mean a teacher cannot deviate from the assigned curriculum to accommodate students' interests and needs. This deviation, however, must be an augmentation of, *not* a substitute for, a productive life in school and in the larger society.

Several staff meetings, with special help if necessary, need to be devoted each year to assist teachers to design ongoing assessment of students' progress toward specified targets. Assessment skills may range from informal validation that students have learned sufficiently to achieve the next task, to formal objective evidence of achievement (tests, projects, portfolios, performances).

The teacher in a nongraded school must become fluent in designing diagnostic procedures and evaluation devices for daily classroom use. Usually this is not part of teacher preparation, so it must be provided in ongoing staff development.

Total school evaluation (summative) to measure the success of a nongraded school should not be limited to academic objectives. Evaluation (both formative and summative) must include valid indicators of physical, social, emotional, and intellectual achievement. Most teachers have neither the time nor the specific skills to develop a defensible school testing program. This procedure requires a sophisticated test constructor and results in criterion-referenced tests. The resulting instruments should be validated by the teachers as measuring the school's objectives.

Standardized tests are useful for identifying the "best" and "worst" as a result of spreading the group. As currently developed and used, they seldom are appropriate for measuring higher level results from excellent curricular objectives and outstanding teaching.

6
Preparation of Parents

WE WILL REPEAT OUR FAILURES OF THE PAST IF WE PLUNGE PARENTS and teachers into nongrading without the necessary preparation. One prerequisite of nongrading is parents' understanding of an organizational scheme that may seem to run counter to their expectations for their child. For example, many parents are eager to have their young child in an older group, believing this is a mark of superiority. When their child is assigned to a classroom that includes younger children, parents sometimes infer that their child is inferior to the other students or object that their older child will be "held back." Sophisticated educators know better; they need to help parents see that when their child works with students of varying ages and abilities in a nongraded classroom, all students have a greater potential for learning.

Easing the Transition

Even though parents know that children in their neighborhood do not play together by ages, they may believe, fostered by years of graded classes, that all students of the same age should be in the same class, learning the same things. Most parents do not consciously realize the tremendous variance in intelligence; academic skills; and physical, emotional, and social characteristics within the same age and grade—even though parents are aware that sister at age 5 was not at all similar to brother at age 5.

Nongrading should begin slowly in a few classes with skilled teachers, not by plunging the whole school into a new system. Parents are accustomed to a class visiting or joining with another class for a special project. Such cooperative arrangements do not make parents apprehensive and can smooth the way for nongrading. Teachers, too, need to become reasonably comfortable, skilled, and committed to nongrading before they are ready to assure parents it is beneficial to their children.

As a few teachers of "adjoining grades" move into the initial phase of nongrading, parents should be informed of their child's assignment to a particular teacher. Then, as two or three teachers begin collaboratively planning and implementing nongrading, they may create instructional groups for students to "visit." These groups should be formed initially on the basis of students' interests. A teacher might say: "Those of you who wish to play kickball, go to Ms. X's group. Those who choose to play basketball will be with Ms. Y. If you wish to work in track and field, go to Mr. Z" or "Decide whether you wish to read adventure stories, tall tales, or science fiction and report to that group."

Groups need not be equal in size; parents and students can become accustomed to the idea of working with others of different ages, grades, and abilities, as well as with different teachers—with no implications about students' abilities and skills. Parents come to realize that groupings are not an indication of their child's intelligence or achievement but an indication that the school is adjusting to their child's interests and needs.

As teachers learn more about their students' skills and needs, custom-tailored instructional groups and cooperative learning groups can be formed to last only as long as appropriate. As soon as teachers are reasonably facile in handling the tailoring of assignments involved in nongrading (skilled teachers have always done this, but not with students of different ages), the teachers determine which class offers the best educational environment and group composition for each learner. Then the student's assignment to a self-contained, nongraded class becomes a reality.

If team teaching is part of the school organizational plan, teachers continue to collaborate in all subject areas and share responsibility for all students in the team; but the teacher who knows the most about a particular student reports that student's progress to the parents. Other ways of communicating with parents include evening parents' meetings, individual conferences, and observational visits to classrooms.

Holding Parent Meetings

One productive way (there are many) to introduce nongrading is to invite parents to a meeting, held at night to accommodate working parents. At this meeting, parents can participate in activities that show the benefits of nongrading. For example, teachers can give parents a set of cards with a description or listing of each student's intellectual, academic, social, emotional, and physical skills—but with no name or age on the card. The parents' task is to sort these cards into classrooms. Parents are amazed to find they have created groups with ages that extended over two or more years. They also learn that a student with 3rd grade math ability might read on either a 2nd or 5th grade level, have 6th grade physical ability, but have the emotional maturity of a much younger child. The preparation of these cards also benefits teachers as they look at students through many dimensions instead of only age, grade level, and IQ.

This "grouping" activity should dispel the notion that all children of the same age belong together and can be taught identical content. Later, when parents see that their child is challenged, supported, and stimulated to greater achievement in a nongraded class, they are convinced of the increased productivity of such a grouping, compared with that of the traditional graded class. When students bring their work home weekly in a portfolio, parents feel well informed about their child's progress; and they can send messages back to the teacher in the portfolio "mailbag." (See Chapter 5 for a discussion of portfolios.)

Regardless of how nongrading is begun, parents should be invited to their child's class meeting, held during the first month of school. In that meeting, usually chaired by the principal, parents are introduced to the rationale and advantages of a *custom-tailored teacher*, or team of teachers, and a *selected peer group* for their child. Staff members to whom a child is assigned describe plans for the year, including what content they anticipate will be included. Teachers and the principal answer parents' questions and concerns and schedule individual conferences for each parent.

Scheduling Parent Conferences

Individual parent conferences, carefully planned and skillfully conducted, allay parents' concerns that their child has been "retained," "accelerated," or "lost" in the group. At the conference, they are reassured that the teacher really knows and cares for their child and is planning for her learning experiences. Parents are amazed to learn of the extreme care being taken by professionals to ensure that each learner's needs are being recognized and accommodated to maximize learning in every area of development.

Parents should be encouraged to bring information to their conference that will help the teacher work increasingly productively with the student. Teachers should list the hours when parents can reach them by phone.

Encouraging Classroom Observations

In addition to conducting parents' meetings and individual conferences, teachers should invite parents to visit the classroom every month or six weeks to learn about and observe their child's participation in a particular subject area. Because reading, writing, and math usually are parents' primary concerns, one of those subjects should be scheduled first.

A short meeting just before each observation alerts parents to what is being learned and practiced and what they should look for in the instructional period. Without such preparation, parents may find observations only "interesting"—or, more often, may misinterpret what happens in the classroom. If they know what the teacher is doing and why, parents come to respect the tremendous complexity of teaching. Creating a knowledgeable, supportive parent group is well worth the additional effort by teachers and the principal.

Teachers should schedule several parent observation days. These should be on different days of the week, a month or six weeks apart, and should focus on different content areas, so that parents can choose convenient times to visit. The observation should be short because parents may feel overwhelmed by the complexities inherent in a long visit, or they may be unable to spend a long time in the classroom on any one day.

Often, inviting parents to view a videotape of classroom activities is better than a "live" demonstration. The teacher can start and stop the tape to explain what is occurring and why. Moreover, students are not self-conscious about being watched by their parents or those of their friends.

Helping Parents Support Their Child's Learning

Both schoolwide and individual class meetings should include discussions of ways parents can support and increase their child's learning, with demonstrations and written suggestions. Most parents are unaware of the current research that undergirds successful teaching. As one of their child's most important teachers, parents need to learn more of the cause-effect relationships between teaching and learning that skilled teachers use daily. Parents are eager to have and grateful for such information, which becomes useful and productive in daily living with their children. Meetings on "how to help your child" may become a routine part of parent association meetings or be scheduled separately throughout the year. Topics should include the traditional academic subjects and the arts, as well as the following:

- Creativity
- Problem solving
- Becoming an independent learner
- Enhancing your child's health
- Self-esteem
- Discipline

A half-hour presentation of just a few techniques, with demonstrations and a brief practice session, can be scheduled several times a year. These "mini-meetings" are much more effective than a long meeting with a full agenda.

When too much information is presented, parents often feel overwhelmed and, therefore, put none of it into practice.

*   *   *

Critical to launching a successful nongraded program is that parents understand the program and support its purpose and procedures. Likewise, teachers must be prepared to conduct the nongraded program comfortably and successfully. The next chapter discusses the preparation of teachers for success in a nongraded school.

7
Preparation of Teachers

A SKILLED TEACHER IN ANY ORGANIZATIONAL SCHEME IS BETTER THAN a mediocre teacher in the best nongraded or team-taught school. The difference is that teachers and administrators in a nongraded school probably have more opportunities—and face more demands—to grow professionally, gaining new skills and insights, rather than continuing previous behavior that may not be as productive as emerging research shows it could become. In a graded school, it's tempting—and the path of least resistance—to follow the graded textbooks and curriculum guides without the stimulation and demand that results from diagnosing and prescribing for students in nongraded classes. Applying those professional skills should result in the provision of more appropriate learning opportunities.

Some teachers may be apprehensive about combining more than one age or grade in their classroom. Their only experiences with "nongrading" may have been in teaching combination classes, where students in different grades were placed together only by necessity, supporting the myth that the single-grade classroom must be a more desirable organization. A few teachers may be reluctant to abandon the security of following decisions that have been made by the textbook or the system. These teachers need time and well-designed staff development opportunities to develop the skills necessary for comfort and success with nongrading. More advanced professional skills are needed when decision making and artistic implementation become a teacher's most important functions.

Most teachers need preparation for the changes in their attitudes and professional approaches called for by the stimulation and demands of nongrading. The provision of *many* staff development opportunities enables teachers to be comfortable with change and reasonably proficient in abandoning age-related goals for a custom-tailored educational prescription. Any organizational system is only as effective as the professionals who implement it. Therefore, successful nongrading (or any organizational scheme) mandates a *continuing* staff development program throughout every year to give teachers the opportunities to constantly enhance their teaching skills, rather than follow a graded textbook or curriculum like a robot. All professionals should continue to develop increasingly effective practices throughout their professional careers. Educators are no exception.

Continuing Education in Content and Pedagogy

Teachers need to learn interdisciplinary content and the effective pedagogy that enables students to achieve success in that content. For example, teachers need to develop fast, accurate techniques for diagnosing each student's current level of functioning in each content area. All students are capable of learning the next thing beyond what they already know. Their only differences are in the size of the "learning step" and speed of achievement. Teachers must know where understanding leaves off and new learning needs to begin.

Constantly increasing professional effectiveness of teachers in both content and pedagogy has become the hallmark of successful schools. Frequent staff meetings should develop proficiency in determining important and worthwhile curricular objectives; diagnosing and prescribing to attain those objectives; acquiring skills to artistically implement that prescription; and using what is now known about carefully selecting and effectively employing many different models in teaching. Meetings on these topics should be routine professional learning opportunities in any successful school, but are critical to a nongraded school. Staff development replaces former, stagnant "teachers' meetings," where professional enhancement was seldom the outcome. (See Hunter 1976a, b; 1982 for sample staff development meetings.)

Teachers must have opportunities *and time* to learn how to task-analyze as a basis for assessing learning and then plan for instruction that incorporates artistically delivered, research-based principles of learning—while still having time outside of school for family, friends, and hobbies. The latter are essential for personal and professional well being.

Staff development can become the weakest aspect of achieving a successful nongraded school, for there still exists a tremendous, unintentional gap between research-based knowledge and practice in some classrooms. This is not the fault of teachers but is a deficit in a profession that used to believe that once a teacher is certified, there is no need to continue to enhance professional proficiency. No other profession operates with that fallacy.

Beginning the Process of Staff Development

A series of staff meetings (not just one!) should introduce the philosophy and concepts of nongrading to dispel the notion of just combining and mixing grade levels. Gene Hall's Concern Based Adoption Model (CBAM) (Hall and Loucks-Horsley 1988) has great relevance here. In a typical school staff, teachers will show different levels of involvement and sophistication. To effect a smooth transition, the administrator must be keenly aware of each teacher's current professional skills and level of concern about new skills. Staff members also need to be "nongraded" for effective professional growth!

The agendas of these introductory staff development meetings should include:

- Philosophy and psychology of nongrading
- Interdisciplinary curriculum; task analysis
- Efficient diagnostic techniques
- Teaching skills and models of teaching
- Assessment (testing) skills
- Reporting to parents
- Learning strategies to develop independent learners

Teachers should attend preparatory staff development programs for at least one year before they begin the nongraded approach. Obviously, this approach to staff development does not end after the introductory year, but is a continuing program that returns again and again to a topic to develop deeper professional understanding and skills. The temptation is to cover something in one meeting and assume it has been learned. Unfortunately, this "quick fix" approach is impossible, given the complexity of emerging research in education.

The objectives of the preparatory sessions are to introduce four professional skills: (1) conducting rapid diagnosis, (2) designing lessons that accommodate more than one level of skill, (3) using effective and efficient "en route" assessment of learning, and (4) teaching to achieve independent learners. Managing a nongraded classroom, or any classroom, can present formidable challenges. Teachers can acquire all these professional skills through staff development while working in the "safety" of a graded class. As the skills become part of their professional repertoire, teachers will realize the power of these practices for accelerating students' achievement. (See Chapters 4 and 5 for detailed discussions of these four skills.)

Conducting Rapid Diagnoses

Teachers at various grade levels need to be reasonably comfortable in using techniques for diagnosing students' entry behaviors; and they must become accustomed to teaching to different levels in a continuum of learning that leads to the school's long-range objectives and goals. As I have already emphasized, excellent teachers have always accommodated differing levels of skill and knowledge among their students. Many of these teachers, however, have worked at an intuitive level, rather than deliberately using articulated professional skills.

Developing Lessons with "Educational Wiggle"

Preparatory staff development programs should also encourage teachers to develop skills in designing lessons with the "educational wiggle" that will accommodate students who need different "catch hold" points in a content area (see Chapter 4).

Learning to Check for Understanding

Teachers should develop proficiency with devices for checking for understanding *while teaching* instead of at the end of a lesson or unit when it's too late to build in the most effective and efficient remediation. If this is not done, the teacher becomes buried under a blizzard of papers to correct, too late for the most effective intervention. Developing skills with student assessments other than paper-and-pencil tests is essential to monitoring students' progress and conserving teachers' time.

Encouraging Independent Learning

Finally, teachers should learn how and what to teach to achieve independent learners, a major objective of a nongraded program. Not only is this skill essential to lifelong learning, but it is critical to the conduct of nongraded classes, where prerequisite skills determine whether students engage in particular learning tasks and where remembered proficiency in any area ends further practice.

"Self-propulsion in learning" is a major nongraded objective, as is "learning how to learn." As students develop proficiency with these skills, they need time to practice without teacher assistance until their independence and self-direction become firmly established. Thereby, the teacher is freed to work with students who are at the initial stage of a new learning task that is inappropriate for the total group but requires maximum teacher guidance. The teacher can also spend time to stimulate and guide more advanced students or to "energize" and inspire average students. Although cooperative learning is an essential part of an *independence* repertoire for every student, initially it requires a great deal of teacher monitoring—more than is necessary for students who are well prepared to engage in individual, independent learning.

Ongoing Staff Development

The move to nongrading, with a diagnostic and prescriptive basis for students' growth in emotional, social, physical, academic, and artistic domains, should begin with only a few excellent teachers. Their experiences, additional insights, and—if they are supported—their subsequent enthusiastic endorsement should encourage others to venture into this new level of professionalism. Plunging the whole school at once into this new organization can result in educational chaos. At the end of two or three years, *with appropriate staff development*, most schools complete the metamorphosis from a traditional graded school to a dynamic, nongraded educational environment designed to optimize each learner's progress and generate parents' enthusiastic endorsement.

Many schools are adopting a nongraded organizational plan because *all* students in nongraded classes, including those at risk of school failure, usually have increased opportunities to make steady, continuous progress, accelerated by an optimal learning environment. Moreover, the move to nongrading equips teachers with enhanced professional skills.

As the philosophy of nongrading begins to be realized either in graded or nongraded classes, the steps toward its achievement should be small and reasonably successful. Teachers who have learned the skills begin by planning nongraded instruction in one content area where the teacher has the most academic security. In some schools, nongrading is begun in art, music, or physical education classes, which are appropriate areas to make adjustments for students whose achievement and ability indicate the need for more or less complex activities. In social studies, science, and writing, developing lessons with "educational wiggle" is possible because much content in these disciplines may not be so dependent on prior understandings or skills.

Successful nongrading and team teaching eventually create an enabling professional environment for both teachers and students, and many teachers never want to leave it. As with a good marriage, there is great satisfaction. The converse is also true—there is nothing worse than a poor marriage, or unsuccessful nongrading. Unsuccessful nongrading or team teaching leaves the participant with a "Never again!" attitude.

Throughout the initial stages of nongrading or team teaching, difficulties and obstacles are sure to arise. Teachers should *not* expect quick success and satisfaction.

Everyone in the school must have support and tolerance, plus the time necessary to solve problems and overcome obstacles. The eventual payoff in terms of everyone's satisfaction and learning is well worth the initial uncertainty and insecurity.

The Payoff of Preparation Efforts

Most teachers, parents, and students who have been prepared to realize the advantages of successful custom-tailored schooling have provided enthusiastic endorsements. Teachers comment, "We may work harder, but we feel more professional; and the boredom and frustration are less."

Parents, at first apprehensive when the accustomed grade-level expectations were removed, have stated:

> We no longer feel our child is an anonymous member of a large parade. At parent conferences, we find the teachers know him as well and often better in certain areas than we do. Most important, our child really enjoys the stimulation at school, feels good about himself as a learner, and resents it if he has to stay home with a cold.

Characteristically, students are the least concerned by the changes from graded to nongraded or from report cards to parent conferences. One boy summarized the situation as follows:

> Grades were only for our parents, anyway. Our teachers let us know how we were doing, but our parents needed grades so they could brag about us or give us heck.

A ten-year-old girl characterized her educational program by stating:

> Every day there are some easier things we need to review, there are lots of medium things we need to learn, and there are a few real hard things that we'll be finding out more about.

These responses are a tribute to the educational soundness of a nongraded school.

8
Teaching to Achieve Independent Learners

THE LEARNER WHO IS IN CHARGE OF HERSELF, WHO CAN MAKE choices and pursue interests, and who can continue learning without the teacher's constant assistance or supervision is likely to become a self-propelling, lifelong learner. To enable students to become independent learners is our paramount goal in education today. In the past, many students have not achieved this goal sufficiently.

Various organizational schemes—open education, team teaching, nongrading, and individualized instruction—as well as different models of teaching, focus on achieving the goal of student independence and self-propulsion in learning. Organizational schemes, however, only create an environment in which this goal can be achieved; no plan ensures that the goal of independence *will* be met. Only skillful teaching can accomplish that.

If learners are to become independent, teachers must assume responsibility for teaching the behavior of "learning independently," just as they teach reading to enable learners to become literate. Some students, of course, learn to read and to work independently with little or no instruction. The majority of learners, however, benefit from the professional assistance a teacher is trained to give.

Formulating an Objective

Let's look briefly at this objective: "The learner works independently and productively on self-selected or assigned activities." This surely is a goal worthy of major teaching effort. In this objective, "independently" means with minimal teacher supervision and assistance, or none;

"productively" means with learning gain for self and no disturbance to others; "self-selected activities" are those chosen from available alternatives; and "assigned" activities are those the teacher determines to be valuable. Figure 8.1 shows seven advantages to the learner that result from teaching to achieve independent learners.

These seven dividends, in themselves, make teaching for independence an essential objective. Additional dividends accrue to the teacher, as shown in Figure 8.2.

Figure 8.1
Teaching Independence: Advantages to Learners

1. Given help in making choices and practicing independent learning, students become decision makers—a skill they will need throughout life.

2. Learners have the practice necessary to develop facility in determining their own activities, following given directions, and completing learning tasks without help.

3. Skilled teachers provide the necessary support, success, or remediation to students who are practicing decision making and independent learning. With such support, students work productively, rather than retreating from decision making and independent learning.

4. Students receive direct feedback from the real world of achievement regarding the success of their independent learning.

5. Learners become responsible for the acquisition, use, care, and storage of materials.

6. Students practice and reinforce their own skills, as they develop new knowledge and skills. They test, strengthen, and improve their own learning strategies for becoming lifelong learners.

7. Students have opportunities to develop skills in working with other students as cooperative members of an independent learning group.

Figure 8.2
Teaching Independence: Advantages to the Teacher

1. By circulating throughout the class and observing learners in independent activities, the teacher secures important information that is available in no other way.

2. Students' learning is no longer completely dependent on the teacher's availability, but can occur without direct assistance or supervision.

3. The teacher becomes available to work *undisturbed* with small groups or individual learners.

4. The teacher has the satisfaction of knowing that students are developing self-direction that will be useful throughout their lives.

Defining Supporting Behavior and Skills_____

If students are to become independent learners, they must acquire certain types of supporting behaviors and skills. A teacher's edict, admonition, or mere provision of opportunities for independence is unlikely to produce the desired behavior. A task analysis reveals prerequisite objectives or types of behavior that learners must acquire to be self-sufficient. A student who is an independent learner shows the following capabilities:

1. Demonstrates the possession of the skills necessary to accomplish the work demanded by the particular independent activity.
2. Discriminates times when choices may be made.
3. Makes an appropriate choice from alternatives when required, and moves from one choice to another without problems.
4. Selects an appropriate place to work.
5. Moves around the room so that others can continue working.
6. Gets necessary materials.
7. Gets started quickly.
8. Follows directions/rules/procedures or creates them for the task.
9. Goes to an appropriate source for help (self, materials, peers, teachers).
10. Works without disturbing others.
11. Works without unnecessary distraction.
12. Returns to the task quickly after an interruption.
13. Responds to the class signal for attention.
14. Uses materials appropriately.
15. Conserves materials.
16. Returns materials to their proper place.
17. Completes tasks according to appropriate criteria.
18. Records any data needed at completion of task.
19. Moves to an appropriate next activity.
20. Abides by classroom routines and rules.
21. Takes care of personal needs according to class procedures.

A learner need not accomplish all these objectives before engaging in independent activities or making choices. Each skill can become a specific teaching objective and be assessed while the student is working—without direct supervision of the academic task but with close supervision of the skills of independence. In fact, *the most effective way to learn these skills is through guided, monitored, and reinforced practice.* Our task analysis suggests the need for activities that encourage independent learning.

Providing Varying Levels of Activities

Three types of independent activities provide students practice in extending self-direction, completing assignments, making choices, and becoming more independent. The activities are increasingly complex. In some classrooms, teachers provide activities at all three levels to accommodate the varying skills of learners. In other classrooms, one or two levels are sufficient.

Type 1 Activities

The main objective of Type 1 activities is to provide *practice in working without direct supervision.* These activities are enjoyable, satisfying, and easily completed; success is highly probable because students have already learned the necessary skills. Usually no new academic learning is involved, and many of these activities are games. Type 1 activities build the foundation of independence—the ability to engage oneself in an activity without adult help or supervision. That ability is learned, practiced, monitored, and reinforced by Type I activities.

The following are examples of simple activities that encourage independence (for students ages 3–13; for older learners, *additional degrees of complexity* should be added):

- Using building materials
- Using modeling clay
- Coloring or painting
- Making collages
- Listening to stories or music at a listening center
- Using individual chalkboards
- Looking at or reading library books
- Working puzzles

• Playing checkers, chess, tic-tac-toe, bingo, and other quiet, familiar games for individuals or small groups.

With these activities, students can practice directing themselves productively.

Type 2 Activities

These activities *give needed practice in already learned academic and artistic skills.* The objective is to increase the learner's ability to work independently and increase speed or fluency (automaticity) in academic or artistic work.

Examples of Type 2 activities follow (simpler activities are listed; those for older or more competent children are the typical tasks assigned by the teacher, such as follow-up work to practice a skill. These are easier for teachers to generate or locate):

• *Math*: Activities that require the appropriate level of addition, subtraction, multiplication, and division: bingo, flash cards, magic squares, worksheets of missing number patterns, simple job cards, or task cards.

• *Reading-Language*:
  – Reading library books
  – Playing games that require word recognition—Quizmo Bingo and Scrabble
  – Using the listening center (following a story or a specific lesson)
  – Practicing writing (letters, words, sentences, paragraphs)
  – Writing stories
  – Copying sentences or completing sentences with illustrations
  – Cutting and pasting sentences or other story elements (for story sequence)
  – Using carefully chosen commercial activities and teacher-made games

Type 3 Activities

These activities (1) encourage creativity and new learning; (2) provide practice in or extend the complexity of learning tasks that are directly related to a current assignment or the student's interests; and (3) give students experience in extending, directing, and monitoring their own learning. Type 3 activities focus on higher cognitive skills, such as analyzing, synthesizing (creating), and evaluating. These more complex and creative independent activities may follow a teacher-directed lesson, take the place of such a lesson, or be student generated. They are designed to accomplish high-level academic or affective objectives. Students working at this level have already shown the ability to work independently through the vehicle of Type 1 and 2 activities. Type 3 activities involve learners in extended self-direction and creative achievement.

The following are examples of students' activities at this level, individually or with a group:

• Follows complex oral or written directions to initiate or complete an open-ended assignment.

• Composes various solutions to difficult questions.

• Composes questions to be answered by others.

• Uses already learned skills to compose different endings, main ideas, and summaries of stories.

• Produces creative compositions or drama, art, and music projects.

• Writes poetry.

• Solves or creates complex (for that student), written word problems in mathematics.

• Reads a library book for characterizations, comparisons, plot, and problem resolution.

• Uses self-selected, prepared material to increase specified skills.

• Initiates or engages in investigation, experimentation, and research projects.

• Works with cooperative groups to initiate, develop, and test creative ideas.

Teaching to Independence

In the previous sections, we performed a task analysis of teaching to independence. First, we formulated a target objective: "The learner works independently and productively on self-selected or assigned activities." We listed the component supporting skills necessary to its achievement; and we described three types of activities that are stepping stones to successful accomplishment. The next step is to combine the results of this task analysis into teaching plans and strategies that will lead to the predictable achievement of these objectives by almost all students. (See Hunter 1985–1988, *Teaching to Develop Independent Learners* [videotapes], for examples of teaching strategies.)

Beginning Stages of Independence

Unless the learners are bringing skills of independence with them, the teacher must start with assignments and choices that enable learners to do things they already know about and enjoy. The teacher can begin with the following assignments and instruction:

1. Set up three to six Type 1 activities from which students may choose.

2. Describe to students what the choices are, where they are located, and how many students are able to participate in each.

3. Give clear directions for (a) selecting an activity; (b) working appropriately; (c) cleaning up when finished; and, if appropriate, (d) making another choice.

4. Ask students to decide which activity they will choose.

5. Ask a few students to model how to go to the activity chosen or get materials for it, then begin to work without teacher help.

6. Dismiss the rest of the students, a few at a time, to make their choices.

7. Circulate during a 15–20-minute period to diagnose students—their needs, interests, and ability to focus and sustain effort. Record the names of students who need help, along with which component of independence they lack. Appropriately reinforce students who demonstrate productive behavior, such as gathering needed materials, focusing on a task, ignoring distractions, moving from one activity to the next, and cleaning up.

8. Give a pretaught signal that indicates there are 2–3 minutes before cleanup.

9. Give a signal for students to stop, clean up, and return to a designated area for evaluation of their

performance in working independently. Reinforce those who respond productively to the signal, and give assistance to those who don't.

If the first day does not go well, the same procedure should be retaught and repeated the next day. If the first day was successful, the teacher can introduce a new Type 2 activity, such as Quizmo (phonics bingo) or Scrabble. The whole class should be taught to play the game, usually by direct instruction and modeling. Then this new activity is added to the choices. The activities suggested are simple examples. Teachers must decide which activities are appropriate for the students in their classrooms.

Within the next few days, other Type 2 activities can be added. Depending on the ability of the learners, the task should vary from copying and illustrating a sentence selected from four models to writing creative riddles or stories and creating a related picture.

Gradually, as students gain proficiency in working independently and develop the skills necessary for making new choices, the teacher eliminates most Type 1 activities and increases Type 2 activities.

After several days of monitoring students' independent activities, the teacher can work with a small instructional group for a *short* time on a practice or review lesson, directing the small group while observing the self-direction of the rest of the class. After the small-group work, the teacher needs to circulate again among the independent workers to reinforce their productive behavior. As students become more proficient in their independence, the teacher can work with several instructional groups. Meanwhile, the other students are productively and independently engaged; as they finish one task, they move to another assignment or activity of their choice with no need for the teacher's help or supervision.

To avoid boredom, extend learning, and continue building skills of independence, new Type 2 and 3 activities should be taught. Activities designed by students should be added to the choices each week or so. As new possibilities are added, old activities should be removed so that students neither lose interest nor face a bewilderingly large assortment of choices.

Some students need special teacher assistance to begin independent activities or to sustain their effort. The teacher can work with these learners in small groups, while monitoring the other, more independent learners. The teacher should help students in the "non-independent" group get started, leave them for a few minutes, and circulate around the rest of the class. Then, returning to the group, the teacher reinforces those who continued to work during this time ("You got a lot done," "You can work well without a teacher"—whatever words are appropriate to the task and the maturity of the learner). The teacher needs to refocus and restart those who didn't sustain their effort ("Show me what you will do next" or "That's right. Now go ahead and I'll be back in a minute to see how you're doing"). Almost all students will eventually respond to this type of remediation, which is *teaching independence* instead of *admonishing* students to work independently.

More Advanced Stages of Independence

When learners are able to work independently, the teacher should provide only Type 2 and 3 choices, including creative contracts, assigned job cards, and student-generated or -designed activities. At times, learners should have no assignments, but be completely responsible for scheduling their time productively. Complex games and experiments should be available to enable students to develop thinking strategies while working productively with friends.

Teachers must formulate questions like those in Figure 8.3, thoughtfully consider their answers, and then provide daily classroom experiences to *teach* learners to function independently. So much is now known in the science that undergirds the art of instruction that a teacher no longer need only hope for independent learners. That outcome can predictably be achieved.

What are the dividends from such an investment of teacher time and energy? The answer is: self-propelling lifelong learners and a teacher with a real sense of professional contribution and accomplishment. The next chapter presents a case study of one school that risked such an investment in encouraging independent learning.

Figure 8.3
Teaching Independence: Questions for Teachers

1. **Content**
   - What skills in language, math, reading, social studies, and other subjects have the students learned well enough to practice independently?
   - What components of more advanced skills do learners need to master?

2. **Organization**
   - Will the students engage in these activities at their usual places (individual desks or tables) or in different areas of the room?
   - Will a particular student work alone, or is she ready to work productively with two or three others?
   - How many activities should be available each day, at what levels of difficulty?
   - Which activities should be changed, and how often?
   - How can materials be stored and organized to be easily accessible to students?

3. **Records**
   - What kinds of records should be kept to monitor students' self-direction?
   - Who will keep these records? Eventually, students should keep their own records; but this, too, is a learned skill that must be taught.
   - Is record keeping easy to maintain? A time-consuming bookkeeping system will drain a teacher's energy and erode teaching and learning time.

4. **Teaching**
   - What are some ways teachers can share their ideas and activities and observe each other to disseminate the artistry and effectiveness of each teacher?
   - What inservice or other educational resources are made available to every teacher?
   - Are teachers encouraged to systematically learn—and incorporate in daily teaching—basic principles related to human learning? These principles promote the accomplishment of any academic, affective, or psychomotor objective.

9
Becoming a Nongraded School: A Case Study

AS PRINCIPAL OF THE UCLA LABORATORY SCHOOL, I INTRODUCED nongrading to a school that, for more than a quarter of a century, had a rigid system of half-grades: a beginning 1st grade (B1) and an advanced 1st grade (A1), a beginning (B2) and an advanced 2nd grade (A2), and so on, up to half-grades B6 and A6. By the end of kindergarten, students' roles were established: the prettiest girl, the "baddest" boy, the cry-baby, the brain, the leader. Six years later, as students progressed to junior high school, they emerged stratified by the same reputation. None had the opportunity of a "fresh start" with a different group who didn't know their prior reputations.

Creating a Few Nongraded Classrooms

As an experimental school, it was our task to introduce a nongraded organizational plan to a very reluctant staff. We began by conducting a series of weekly staff development meetings, and then instituted a few nongraded, self-contained classrooms. We matched students to teachers and peer groups to provide the optimum educational environment possible for each learner.

At first, teachers used their most comfortable teaching styles with their nongraded classes, making few adjustments to the needs of individual students for particular teaching styles. Because each group had been constituted to work well together and with that particular teacher, teachers did not have to deal with many of the "indigestible lumps" that are present in most classrooms.

Students' "enemies" were not present to distract or deter them from work. Each classroom included *clusters* of students who needed similar learning tasks (social, physical, or academic). Consequently, a teacher's energy was not dissipated by designing a learning opportunity for only one student with needs differing from those of other students.

In these self-contained, nongraded classrooms, teachers began to realize that age and grade level were not accurate predictors of students' learning needs. They found, as we expected, that some younger students could read, write, spell, hypothesize, or play ball better than some of the older ones. They also found that some of the more reticent older students bloomed as they showed off their skills when helping others. Soon teachers began to ignore age or grade level and focus instead on each student's needs and the type of group, environment, and teaching style in which those needs (social, emotional, intellectual, academic, and physical) could best be met.

At the beginning, we did not expect teachers to feel competent, comfortable, or satisfied with nongrading. The inevitable complaints and wishes to go "back to the way we were" were met by, "You may be right, but we'll never know unless we give it time to work and for us to learn." As teachers developed their skills, complaints turned into tolerance, then into enthusiasm and excitement with the professional intoxicant of their own growth and the students' increased levels of success. This metamorphosis did not happen overnight or with all teachers. Two teachers transferred out of the school at the end of the first year. The others, to varying degrees, began to look forward to the professional growth they were experiencing during what formerly had been routine staff meetings that dealt only with administrivia. As one teacher put it, "It's the first time I've felt like a truly effective professional who knew what I was doing and why I was doing it!"

The Beginning of Team Teaching

At the beginning of the second year, I asked for volunteers to try team teaching with nongraded classes.

Three teachers volunteered, while the rest of the staff breathed a sigh of relief that they had been "spared."

The three teachers had diverse teaching styles and areas of competence. One woman was a warm, nurturing teacher with skills in language arts and social studies. The other woman was a dynamic, exciting teacher with special skills in the arts. The third, a man, was a former U.S. Air Force pilot with skills in math, science, and physical education. Together, they comprised a galaxy of expertise and a pharmacy of teaching styles.

At first, the team members thought "departmentally," expecting to teach only their specialties, not *all* subjects. They were not used to thinking collaboratively or contributing to and learning from the skills of the others. Each was assigned the major responsibility for the overall design of curricular areas in which that team member had skill. Other team members provided correction and augmentation to the plan; and all teachers worked together in diagnosing the learning needs of students and assigning them to instructional groups—the foundation for the subsequent educational program and for teacher growth.

Teaming began slowly, with a great deal of support and assistance from the principal. First, I called on the art, music, and drama/dance specialists for help in adjusting the master schedule. The specialists, who typically worked with students one day a week, combined their schedules to take all students in the team-taught class for an hour every day and thus free the teachers for a joint planning period. The plan worked like this: a third of the 80 students had art for one hour every day for a week, a third had music, and the rest attended drama/dance. Then the groups rotated.

Leaving the "once a week, dribble, dribble, drip" schedule initially caused concern among the specialists—until they saw how much more they could accomplish and how much less the students forgot when instruction and practice were consistent for five days. Eventually, the whole school adopted a schedule of three weeks of one specialization, then a time to practice independently or under the supervision of the regular teacher, then three weeks of another area. Students learned skills and techniques well enough in those three weeks that they could sustain and even extend their skills during the "in-between" practice periods.

Those daily planning periods, when the specialists became responsible for students, were life savers for our team teachers. I attended many of the planning meetings to contribute suggestions or help resolve problems.

To help parents and students become accustomed to the innovation of team teaching, students originally were assigned to just one of the teachers. Groups were first combined in the physical education period, which all three classes shared. The program was organized by the male teacher, but taught by all three teachers. At the beginning, some students played games of their choice, with observation and supervision by one teacher, while the other two teachers worked with smaller groups to diagnose physical skills, cooperation, and sportsmanship. Before long, the physical education program became a custom-tailored learning opportunity; students worked on individual skills, team games, and social-emotional growth in an environment designed to maximize learning.

The teachers' next combinational move was in mathematics, where it was easiest to diagnose computational and reasoning skills. Again, the groups were not stratified, with one teacher teaching the "best" and another the "worst" students. At first, the teacher most proficient in math took charge of the remedial group to determine how to accelerate their learning. The other teachers each taught a greater number of students in both higher and lower groups, but with no remedial students.

After a couple of weeks, groups were reassigned as teachers discovered what the less able students needed to learn. Some students simply did not have the necessary math concepts. Others could reason well, but lacked computational skills or reasonable automaticity with number facts. At this point, the most proficient teacher and the accelerated math students worked together to design and implement a program tailored to give students a great deal of responsibility for applying math to new situations and to develop independent self-propulsion into new learning. Each teacher's math groups might last two weeks or two months. Composition of the groups changed as students' needs or the objectives changed. Frequently, students were grouped by their interests or their own choices.

A few students had difficulty adjusting to changing teaching styles and different groups. Initially, a student with this difficulty remained with one teacher, who helped the student with adjustments to the group. Then the student went to a different teacher for the subject area in which the student felt most comfortable. Little by little, students with adjustment problems were "fed out" to different teachers and groups. Eventually, these students developed competence and reasonable success in all their assigned groups.

During the second month of school, we held a parent meeting at night to explain the procedure, purpose, and advantages of what was happening in the children's school experiences. A few parents showed cautious, tentative acceptance. Many had already heard enthusiastic endorsements by their own children: "It's really neat to have different teachers and groups. There's always someone I like. I'm making new friends and learning a lot."

The Gradual Spread of Teaming

At periodic staff meetings, the other teachers in the lab school were kept informed of the advantages and problems of teaming. They often had excellent suggestions and sometimes offered help with materials or supervision. A few teachers were stimulated to begin planning with colleagues, encouraged and supported by the principal, and the following year requested a teaming assignment. At the end of the second year, most teachers (not all) were teaming, and most parents (not all) were requesting that their children be assigned to a team.

By now, we had learned the two critical attributes of a successful team:

1. Teachers must be willing to share their skills and materials and to learn new skills that enhance the educational program for students.

2. Teachers must willingly share the adulation that is extended to "my teacher" by most students.

One of our original team members could not accept this extensive sharing. She, being an excellent teacher, had relished her reputation among students and parents as "the best" teacher in the school. The following year, she withdrew from the team and requested a self-contained classroom. Later, she left the school.

Eventually, the staff created an internationally famous, nongraded, team-taught school. Some educators, interested in nongrading but skeptical of how to find planning time, protest, "But we don't have specialists. We can't arrange planning time." Yet it's amazing how much time can be made available in other creative ways. For example, the school can hold a weekly assembly that includes an educational film, followed by a written or pictorial summary by each student. This activity requires minimal supervision—once students have been *taught* the necessary skills. More time is freed when several classes meet in the schoolyard with assigned or chosen activities requiring minimal (but adequate) supervision. Or several classes can combine for a story or program. Parents, *with training*, can provide excellent experiences for students or supervise their independent work within the requirement of adequate supervision. Aides or the principal can occasionally release teachers for planning. In addition, much can be accomplished by small groups of teachers in the times designated for staff meetings or preparation periods. I have worked with teachers under many school conditions; planning time can be found if the school staff deem it important.

The dividends of such well-planned, structured time are immense. It is professional cooperative learning of the highest order. But, as with all cooperative learning, participants must have the skills necessary to work together. Purposes and objectives must be well planned, and teachers must be well prepared to engage in team planning. The objective of *enhanced educational opportunities for all students* must take precedence, but teachers must still be responsive to individual preferences and needs.

Epilogue

After a few years, when the lab school teachers had acquired the skills of teaming in a nongraded school, we attempted to determine what such effective teachers could accomplish in a self-contained, nongraded classroom. The teachers balked. Once they had experienced the advantages of teaming, none wished to return to the loneliness of a self-contained class. With pressure, two teachers reluctantly agreed to try it, "but only for a year!"

Our questions were never answered because those two teachers planned together before and after school and surreptitiously "traded students" when they felt it was indicated.

Though nongrading and team teaching demand advanced professional skills, the satisfaction of accelerated growth for both students and teachers makes the outcomes well worth the effort.

References

Cox, J. (1983). "Continuous Progress and Nongraded Schools." *Gifted Education International* 2, 1: 61–65.

Gardner, H. (1983). *Frames of Mind: The Theory of Multiple Intelligences.* New York: Basic Books.

Goodlad, J.I., and R.H. Anderson. (1959; 1963, 1987). *The Non-Graded Elementary School.* New York: Teachers College.

Hall, G., and S. Loucks-Horsley. (March 1988). *Concern Based Adoption Model (CBAM): Procedures for Adopting Educational Innovation Programs.* Austin, Tex.: Research and Development Center for Teacher Education, University of Texas. (Paper presented at a meeting of the American Educational Research Association).

Hunter, M. (1976a). *Aide-ing in Education.* El Segundo, Calif.: TIP Publications, P.O. Box 514, El Segundo, CA 90245. Telephone: (310) 322-8437.

Hunter, M. (1976b). *Improved Instruction.* El Segundo, Calif.: TIP Publications.

Hunter, M. (1978). *Parent-Teacher Conferencing.* El Segundo, Calif.: TIP Publications.

Hunter, M. (1982). *Mastery Teaching.* El Segundo, Calif.: TIP Publications.

Hunter, M. (1985–1988). *Teaching to Develop Independent Learners.* (Videotapes). Special Purpose Films, 416 Rio del Mar Blvd., Aptos, CA 95003. Telephone: (408) 688-6320.

Katz, L.G., et al. (1990). *The Case for Mixed-Age Grouping in Early Education.* Washington, D.C.: National Association for the Education of Young Children. (ERIC Clearinghouse on Elementary and Early Childhood Education, Urbana, Ill.; ED326302 PS018894).

Malsam, M. (April 1980). "Trends in Education: A New Look at IGE Systems." *Curriculum Review* 19, 2: 110–113.

Maxwell, L. (1986). *Making the Most of Ability Grouping.* Research in Brief. Washington, D.C.: Office of Educational Research and Improvement.

Rudisill, E. M., et al. (January 1982). "Nongraded Instruction, Mathematics Ability, and Mathematics Achievement in Elementary Schools." *Journal for Research in Mathematics Education* 13, 1: 61–66.

Wiersma, W. (April 1986). *Individually Guided Education: An Alternative Form of Schooling.* Paper presented at the Annual Meeting of the American Educational Research Association, San Francisco.